A I R W A R A R C H I V E

HEINKEL He 111

THE EARLY YEARS – FALL OF FRANCE, BATTLE OF BRITAIN AND THE BLITZ

CW00954327

A I R W A R A R C H I V E

HEINKEL He 111

THE EARLY YEARS – FALL OF FRANCE, BATTLE OF BRITAIN AND THE BLITZ

Chris Goss

FRONTLINE BOOKS

HEINKEL He 111
The Early Years – Fall of France, Battle of Britain and the Blitz

This edition published in 2017 by Frontline Books,
an imprint of Pen & Sword Books Ltd,
47 Church Street, Barnsley, S. Yorkshire, S70 2AS

ISBN: 978-1-84832-483-1

CIP data records for this title are available from the British Library

For more information on our books, please visit
www.frontline-books.com,
email info@frontline-books.com
or write to us at the above address.

Printed and bound by CPI Group (UK) Ltd, Croydon, CR0 4YY

Typeset in 10/12 Avenir

CONTENTS

ACKNOWLEDGEMENTS

I would like to thank the following for their assistance in compiling this book: Peter Cornwell, Robert Forsyth, the late Manfred Griehl, the late Michael Payne, Alfred Price, Bernd Rauchbach, and Ken Wakefield.

THE HEINKEL He 111
The Luftwaffe's Workhorse

The Heinkel He 111 was probably the most distinctive German bomber of the Second World War. A pre-war cargo aircraft, the military variants served from the first to the last days of the war in all of Germany's campaigns and offensives, and in bomber, reconnaissance, training, test and evaluation, torpedo and transport roles, even being used as a launch platform for the V-1 flying bomb.

EARLY DEVELOPMENT

Because the Treaty of Versailles placed severe restrictions on German aircraft development and production (particularly in terms of military aircraft), the future after the First World War for German aircraft designers and manufacturers looked bleak. However, in 1922, Ernst Heinkel, who had previously worked for the LVG, Albatros, Hansa-Brandenburg and Caspar-Werke aircraft companies, formed the Heinkel-Flugzeugwerke company at Warnemünde on the edge of the Baltic. Customers were initially hard to come by but he was successful in obtaining contracts with Sweden and Japan. The rise of Adolf Hitler and the Nazi Party (Ernst Heinkel was a Party member) presented Heinkel with the opportunity to develop new aircraft.

In the early 1930s, Heinkel announced the Company's intention to produce a passenger aircraft, the design and development of which was given to Siegfried and Walter Günter. The first aircraft to appear was the single-engine four-passenger Heinkel He 70 which could reach speeds of 390 km/h (230 mph). The He 70 then spawned what was essentially a twin-engine version of itself. When the Dornier Do 17 proved itself a better and faster passenger aircraft than the He 70, Heinkel put considerable effort into developing an improved machine, which became the He 111.

The first He 111 flew at the end of February 1935, powered by BMW VI liquid-cooled engines which were poor compared to the Junkers Jumo 205-powered Junkers Ju 86, considered by many to be the He 111's most serious rival. However, re-equipping the He 111 with Daimler-Benz DB600 engines turned the tables and gave it a considerable advantage over its rival. As a result, the He 111 became the favoured civilian, and quickly afterwards, military aircraft for pre-war Germany.

INTO PRODUCTION

The second production He 111 entered service with Deutsche Luft Hansa (DLH) in 1936, initially designated the He 111C. The upgraded version would be the He 111G which had a number of improvements, including wing modifications and a series of different engines. By 1937, a total of twelve He 111Cs and Gs were in service with DLH, though it was at this stage that attention switched entirely to the design's military role.

The first military version was the He 111A which had a machine-gun in the nose, another on the upper fuselage and a retractable ventral 'dustbin' turret. However, once bombs were loaded, performance was seriously reduced and, as a result, the He 111B was introduced. This was powered by DB600 engines and also featured minor changes to the nose and ventral gun positions. This appealed to the Luftwaffe which placed orders for 300 B-1s, the first of which was completed in January 1937. However, Heinkel was unable to meet demand which resulted in Arado, Dornier and Junkers being used as sub-contractors, ironically all of them being competitors of Heinkel.

The next development was the He 111E. Powered by Jumo 211 engines, this variant was produced in time to serve with the Legion Condor in Spain in 1938. Later sub-variants saw the fitting of external bomb racks, modified internal bomb racks and an increased fuel capacity.

The F series then saw minor design changes, including the fitting of Jumo 211 engines, after which Heinkel developed the He 111J which was intended as a maritime bomber. However, as a result of disagreements between the Luftwaffe and Kriegsmarine as to who 'owned' maritime combat aircraft and how they would be operated, most Js ended up as trainers.

INTO WAR

The more recognisable He 111 was the He 111P which, without the stepped cockpit of the earlier versions, first flew in January 1938. The new glazed nose, updated DB601 engines, additional defensive armament, armour plating, external bomb racks and more aerodynamic dorsal and ventral gun positions were the main changes.

The He 111P was widely used in Poland, Norway, the Battle of France and Battle of Britain but its vulnerability to modern fighters was soon evident. This resulted in the He 111P-4 sub-variant being produced which increased the machine's defensive armament from three machine-guns up to a total of seven. However, the Luftwaffe now needed DB601 engines for its fighters which resulted in the He 111 P being fitted with Jumo 211 engines and being re-designated the He 111H, all but identical to the P-4 apart from the engines.

The He 111H was the ultimate He 111 variant, serving in various guises until the end of the war. It had up to twenty-two sub-variants (H-1 to H-23 but skipping H-13, H-17 and H-19) which in addition to standard bomber roles included a torpedo bomber (the H-6), balloon cutter (H-8 to H-10), glider tug (H-11/R2, H-16/R2), glider bomb carrier (H-12), Blohm & Voss 246 glide bomb launch pad (H-15), pathfinder (H-16/R2, H-18), paratrooper carrier (H-20/R1), cargo carrier and glider tug (H-20/R2), V-1 launcher (H-22).

Both the He 111P and He 111H were actively used in the opening campaigns of the Second World War, albeit the arrival of the more modern and faster Junkers Ju 88 saw a number of He 111 units, such as *Kampfgeschwader* 51 (*KG* 51), being re-equipped with the Ju 88 by the summer of 1940. Furthermore, the increase in the He 111's defensive armament also necessitated increasing its normal crew of a pilot, observer, radio operator and flight engineer (the latter three also acting as gunners) by another gunner. However, as the Luftwaffe's failure in the Battle of Britain resulted in daylight operations being replaced predominantly by night missions, the He 111 would enjoy a brief respite and operate successfully as a pathfinder using the X and Y-Verfahren.

In June 1941, the majority of the Luftwaffe moved eastwards to participate in Operation *Barbarossa* – the invasion of the Soviet Union. At the same time, more German air assets were needed in the Mediterranean. This meant that the He 111 became a very rare visitor to the skies over Britain, with it being deployed more in the anti-shipping role, especially in the Mediterranean.

The development of the torpedo role was given to 1 Staffel/*Kampfgruppe* 126 (later re-designated 1/*KG* 28) and in November 1940, three crews flying from Nantes in western France, those commanded by *Oberleutnant* Helmut Lorenz, *Oberleutnant* Josef Saumweber and *Oberleutnant* Friedrich Müller, began to carry out experimental torpedo missions in the seas around Great Britain. Their first mission was stated as being 9 November 1940 during which the He 111H-4 'Luft Torpedo Flugzeug' as it was called, and flown by Lorenz, was shot down by a Bristol Blenheim of 236 Squadron.

The He 111H-6 would continue to be used in the maritime reconnaissance and attack role over the Bay of Biscay (before being replaced by the Focke Wulf Fw 200 and Dornier Do 217) but the torpedo-equipped He 111s, the role now taken on by II/*KG* 26, would have more success in the Mediterranean.

Over Russia, it was soon discovered that the He 111's restricted range and bomb load (the He 111H-6 had an endurance of just under 1,500 miles and a bomb load of less than 4,500lbs) prevented it from being a true strategic or long-range bomber capable of reaching targets well inside the Soviet Union. Its replacement, the Heinkel He 177, was plagued by development problems and

despite the He 177 flying its initial missions at the end of 1943, the He 111 had to soldier on, the last production month for the type being as late as September 1944. By this stage of the war, however, the Luftwaffe's bomber force was a shadow of its former self, Germany concentrating production on fighter aircraft to defend the Reich.

OPERATIONAL HISTORY

A good illustration of how the He 111 was used throughout the war is provided through the career of an NCO Beobachter (Observer) by the name of Josef Schmauz.

Schmauz joined his unit, 6/*KG* 53, in France at the end of 1940 when he flew night bombing missions over Britain before moving to the Russian Front in June 1941. On 29 June 1941, whilst flying a daylight bombing raid in a He 111H-4, he and his crew were shot down by Soviet fighters and crashed behind enemy lines. All on board survived the crash without injury, but only Josef and one other crewman returned to German lines; the other three, although they surrendered, were never seen again.

With a new pilot, Schmauz continued to fly missions over Russia. On 20 January 1943, his crew was flying resupply missions into Gumrak in support of German troops surrounded at Stalingrad when his He 111H-6 had its fuselage all but severed in half by artillery; he and his crew were lucky to get out on another He 111.

Worse followed. On 31 July 1943, Schmauz's He 111H-16 was shot down by anti-aircraft fire, though all on board baled out successfully. Schmauz went back to Germany to be an instructor before returning to operational flying in 1944. After D-Day in June 1944, his unit was flying resupply missions from Rouvres in France with the He 111H-20. On 28 August 1944, they were recalled to Germany where they undertook training to fly missions launching the V-1 flying bomb.

Unfortunately for them, they were bounced by American fighters, and seven He 111H-20s, all of which were carrying ground crew, were shot down. In all thirty-four aircrew and ground crew were killed and twenty-two, including Schmauz, were wounded.

By mid-July 1944, the Allied advance began to take ground used by the Germans as V-1 launch sites. Consequently, the Luftwaffe began night launches of the V-1 under-slung from He 111s in an attempt to continue what was known as Operation *Rumpelkammer* ('Junk Room'), the flying-bomb assault on the UK. Initial missile-launching operations were flown by III/*KG* 3 from Venlo in Holland, launching some 300 V-1s at London, a further ninety at Southampton and about twenty at Gloucester by the end of August 1944. After a lull while III/*KG* 3 transferred from Venlo to bases in Schleswig-Holstein in north-west Germany, where they would join and later be subsumed into KG 53, operations resumed on 16 September 1944.

Sporadic attacks were made on most nights up to the end of the month with a total of 177 missiles being despatched, predominantly against London. This increased to 282 in October and 316 in November 1944, by which time Leeds and Manchester were also targets. The hazardous nature of the operations, though, took a heavy toll on *KG* 53 with seventeen aircraft being lost either to RAF night fighters, accidents or even the V-1s detonating prematurely after take-off.

These air launch operations finally terminated on 14 January 1945, by which stage *KG* 53 had lost another twelve H-16s or H-20s. From then on the He 111 was used purely in the transport role, but most would be grounded due to a lack of fuel, spares and crews or overwhelming Allied air superiority.

CURIOUS TWIN

There was one further version of the He 111

– the He 111Z or Zwilling (Twin). The joining of two He 111H-6 fuselages and the fitting of five engines allowed this curious aircraft to tow the massive Messerschmitt 321 glider, albeit putting engines on the glider resulted in the Me 323 and no need for a tug for it to get airborne. It is believed that ten Zwillings were produced, generally being used for towing the more normal Gotha 242 and on transport missions.

Most of the Zwillings were lost in accidents or during attacks on airfields but one, *werke nummer* 2704 from 4/Luftlandegeschwader 2, together with the two Gotha 242s it was towing, was shot down by a Mosquito of 418 Squadron near Tavaux airfield in France on 26 February 1944; the successful Canadian pilot, on seeing the twin fuselage, even considered filing a claim for two He 111s.

There was an intention to use the He 111Z-2 as a launch platform for the Henschel 293 glide bomb and the He 111Z-3 as a strategic reconnaissance aircraft but these schemes were never pursued.

EXPORT

Pre-war, He 111F-1s and G-1s were bought by the Turkish Air Force and another twelve He 111As were bought by the Chinese. At the end of the Spanish Civil War, Spain kept a number of the older variants formerly used by the Legion Condor. During the Second World War, some of Germany's allies, namely Hungary, Bulgaria, Slovakia and Romania, operated the He 111s and a number were then used in the civilian role after the war.

From 1945 to 1956, the Spanish aircraft manufacturer Construcciones Aeronáuticas SA produced the CASA 2.111. To say they were identical to the He 111 is incorrect, but they did share the same airframe in appearance and the earlier aircraft did have Jumo 211 engines but it was more normal for them to be powered by Rolls-Royce Merlins. A total of 236 were produced. This aircraft was withdrawn from service in 1973 but not before having been used with great success in the filming of the epic *Battle of Britain*.

SURVIVORS

A total of just over 6,500 He 111s were built between 1935 and 1944, but only four genuine examples exist – a He 111E-3 in Madrid, a He 111H-2 in Berlin, a He 111P-1 in Norway and a He 111H-20 in the RAF Museum in London. A cockpit section of a He 111H-6 is known to exist in Sweden. About fourteen CASA 2.111s exist around the world, in storage, on display or in various stages of renovation.

GLOSSARY

Adj	Adjutant
Aufklärungsgruppe	Reconnaissance Wing
Bordfunker	Radio Operator
Beobachter	Observer
Bordmechaniker	Flight Engineer
Bordschütz	Air Gunner
Deutsches Kreuz in Gold	German Cross in Gold award
Do	Dornier
Ehrenpokal	Goblet of Honour-awarded for outstanding achievements in the air war
Eiserne Kreuz	Iron Cross (came in First and Second Class)
Ergänzungs	Training
Eskadra Myśliwska	Fighter squadron (Polish Air Force)
Feindflug	Operational flight
Feldwebel	Flight Sergeant
Fern	Long range
Flak	Anti-aircraft fire
Flieger	Aircraftman
Fliegerführer Atlantik	Air Commander for the Atlantic region
Fluzeugführer	Pilot
Flugzeugführerschule	Flying school
Freie Jagd	Free hunting fighter sweep
Frontflugspange	Mission Clasp awarded for operational flights
Führer	Leader
Gefreiter	Leading Aircraftman
Generalfeldmarschall	Air Chief Marshal
Geschwader	Group consisting three Gruppen commanded by a Geschwader Kommodore
Gruppe	Wing consisting three Staffeln; commanded by a Gruppen Kommodore. The Gruppe number is denoted by Roman numerals
Hauptmann	Flight Lieutenant/Captain

Ia	Operations Officer
Jabo	Fighter-bomber
Jagd	Fighter
Jagdgeschwader	Fighter Group
Jagdgruppe	Fighter Wing
Ju	Junkers
Kampfgeschwader	Bomber Group
Kampfgeschwader zur besonderen Verwendung	Normal designation for a transport unit
Kette	Three aircraft tactical formation similar to RAF vic
Kriegsmarine	German Navy
Lehrgeschwader	Technical Development Flying Group
Leutnant	Pilot Officer/Second Lieutenant
Luftflotte	Air Fleet
Major	Squadron Leader/Major
Me	Messerschmitt
Nachtrichtenoffizier	Communications Officer
Oberfeldwebel	Warrant Officer
Obergefreiter	Senior Aircraftman/Corporal
Oberleutnant	Flying Officer/First Lieutenant
Oberst	Group Captain/Colonel
Oberstleutnant	Wing Commander/Lieutenant Colonel
Plutonowy	Sergeant (Polish Air Force rank)
RAF	Royal Air Force
Reichsluftfahrtministerium	German Air Ministry
Reichsmarschall	Marshal of the Air Force
Ritterkreuz	Knight's Cross
Ritterkreuz mit Eichenlaub	Knight's Cross with Oakleaves
Rotte	Two aircraft tactical formation; two Rotten made a Schwarm; commanded by a Rottenführer
Rottenflieger	Wingman
Schlacht	Ground attack
Schwarm	Four aircraft tactical formation commanded by a Schwarm Führer
Seenotflugkommando	Air Sea Rescue Detachment
Sonderführer	Rank usually given to War Reporters
Sonderstaffel	Special Staffel
Stab	Staff or HQ formation in which Gruppen Kommodore and Geschwader Kommodore flew.
Stabsfeldwebel	Senior Warrant Officer
Staffel	Squadron (twelve aircraft); commanded by a Staffel Kapitän. The Staffel number is denoted by Arabic numerals
Technischer Offizier	Technical Officer
Unteroffizier	Sergeant
Werke nummer	Serial Number
Wettererkundungsstaffel	Weather reconnaissance unit (of squadron strength)
Zerstörer	Destroyer/Heavy fighter
Zerstörergeschwader	Heavy Fighter Group

Dr Ernst Heinkel (far right) standing in front of an early production model Heinkel He 70, which in turn was a direct ancestor of the He 111. The He 70 would usually be coloured white with national markings on the tail in black in a white disc on a red banner; the front was generally black with white writing. Although from the front the He 70 bears little resemblance to the He 111, from the rear the tail and fuselage appear very similar. Though the prototype He 70, which first flew on 1 December 1932, was found to have excellent performance, setting eight world records for speed over distance, and reaching a maximum speed of 222 mph, the type had a relatively brief commercial career before it was replaced by designs which could carry more passengers.

Above: On the ground in the centre of this picture is the second prototype He 111. In service with DLH (Deutsche Lufthansa), it was coded D-ALIX and named *Rostock*. In the air above is another early He 111, in this D-AXAV, which was named *Köln*. To the far right are a number of He 70s, the nearest being coded D-UBAF and showing the similarities in the rear fuselage to the He 111.

Opposite: A Heinkel He 111 in service with DLH showing mail being loaded through the nose door. Whilst work commenced on a military version, the evolution of the commercial model for the DLH had continued

in the Rostock factory. The summer of 1936 saw the beginning of the assembly of six pre-production planes, which received the designation He 111C-0. By the end of 1936 all six C-0s had been built and each aircraft duly received its own name. The six were: He 111 C-01 *Nurnberg* (D-AMES); He 111 C-02 *Leipzig* (D-AQYF); He 111 C-03 *Köln* (D-AXAV); He 111 C-04 *Konigsberg* (D-ABYE); He 111 C-05 *Breslau* (D-AQUA); and He 111 C-06 *Karlsruhe* (D-ATYL).

After being used for a short time on local routes, DLH declared that the He 111C was too expensive and not economical. The He 111C program was duly cancelled and all six

pre-production C-planes were allocated to the so-called 'Prestigious Routes', namely Berlin-Hanover-Amsterdam, Berlin-Nuremberg-Munich, and Cologne-Dortmund-Berlin. In time, two of the six – He 111C-01 and He 111C-05 – were used as special courier aircraft in the southern Atlantic.

In mid-1937 He 111C-03 was handed over to a secret reconnaissance unit named 'Kommando Rowehl', which was commanded by *Oberstleutnant* Theodore Rowehl. In effect, Kommando Rowehl was a special photographic reconnaissance unit, whose aircraft carried civil registrations and which performed clandestine photographic sorties over the United Kingdom, France and the Soviet Union. Following the outbreak of war in 1939, the number of DLH's commercial routes that continued to operate were minimal. The He 111C, as well as another transport version, the He 111G, was still used on the Berlin-Danzig-Konigsberg route, as well as a few times on the Moscow-Berlin route. Indeed, just after the invasion of Poland all of DLH's He 111Cs and He 111Gs were requisitioned by the Luftwaffe. These aircraft were fitted with military radio equipment and defensive armament. In the next few years the He111C was used by the Luftwaffe as a general liaison aircraft.

Above: A selection of brand new He 111Bs showing the modified nose developed for military use. The Heinkel He 111B was the first version of this aircraft to be ordered by the Luftwaffe. The first He 111B made its maiden flight in the autumn of 1936, whilst the first batch rolled out of the factory, at Rostock, that summer. Amounting to seven aircraft in total, these B-0 pre-production aircraft were given the werke nummern 1431 to 1437. After a number of improvements, the Reichsluftfahrtministerium (the German Ministry of Aviation, which was responsible for the development and production of all aircraft developed, designed and built in Germany during the existence of the Third Reich – and usually just referred to as the RLM) went on to order a production run of 300 He 111B-1s, the first of which was delivered in January 1937.

Opposite top: A He 111B of an unidentified Luftwaffe unit. Like many bombers of the late 1930s, the He 111 was faster than contemporary fighter aircraft when it was developed. In the case of the He 111 this was partly responsible for the adoption of inadequate defensive armament. Aside from the nose modifications described previously, another significant change made for production examples of this version was the replacement of the underpowered BMW VI engines with Daimler Benz DB 600C engines, resulting in marked improvements in top speed and overall performance of the design. Though these aircraft are painted in a military camouflage scheme, they still carry civilian registration letters.

Opposite bottom: He 111B coded SE+GP. Visible underneath just behind the trailing edge is the retractable ventral 'dustbin' turret. The aircraft's werk nummer is stencilled on the tail above the national marking and the aircraft exhibits the standard bomber splinter camouflage.

Above: Groundcrew working on the Daimler Benz DB600 engines of a He 111B. The lump under the nose is for the bomb sight.

Opposite: A He 111B of *Kampfgruppe* 88 (*K*88) serving as part of the Legion Condor during the Spanish Civil War. This particular aircraft carries the code 25-52. *K*88 was initially equipped with the Junkers Ju 52 in the auxiliary bomber role, re-equipping with the He 111 from July 1937. It was 4.Staffel that was the first to complete this conversion, the others having done so by July the following year.

Opposite: This picture shows what are thought to be He 111E-1s of *K*88 taken at Ávila in Spain. Note that the unit's eagle and bomb insignia has been painted on the tail as opposed to the fuselage. The nearest aircraft has the *werke nummer* 342 stencilled on the nose. Unlike the fighter units of the Legion Condor, *K*88 normally kept its staffel grouped together for maximum effectiveness and concentration during its bombing missions – one of which included the bombing of Guernica on 26 April 1937. In keeping with the Luftwaffe's doctrine at the time, most of *K*88's missions were in tactical support of ground forces.

Above: The distinctive artwork applied to the tail of a He 111B flown by *Leutnant* Helmut Fuhrhop of 4/*K*88. It is Fuhrhop's dog, which appears to be a Scottish terrier, that is

depicted. Named Peter, it was killed during an attack on a railway line at Sagunto, a town in eastern Spain some twenty miles north of Valencia, on 13 June 1938. During the sortie Fuhrhop's Heinkel was attacked by Republican fighters, returning to base with no less than sixty-five bullet holes. Fuhrhop's service in the Luftwaffe continued well into the Second World War; a successful bomber pilot, he was awarded the Ritterkreuz. He was shot down by RAF fighters on 29 February 1944, over Seboncourt in France, whilst commanding I/*KG* 6; he, his crew and his two dogs, Chica and Ciro, were all killed.

Above: This He 111B-1 from *K*88, which appears to have suffered a landing accident, has the name *Pedro* painted on the nose. During its deployment in Spain, the He 111 was often referred to by the nickname *Pedro*, which in turn was derived from the false passports issued to the volunteer German personnel of the Legion Condor.

Right: A He 111B of *K*88. Note the tarpaulin on the nose and cockpit. The emblem seen here is similar to that seen on He 111s of 4/*KG* 53 during the Second World War.

Opposite top: A He 111E of the Legion Condor being bombed-up for another mission. The E-1 variant began to roll off the production lines in February 1938, just in time for a small number to serve in Spain. Whilst the bomb bays in early versions of the He 111 were fitted with four bomb racks, in later versions these were replaced by eight modular standard bomb racks designed to carry one SC 250 or four SC 50 bombs each in a nose-up orientation.

Opposite bottom: This He 111B of an unidentified unit is pictured with its undercarriage having apparently sunk into the ground. This image provides an excellent view of the the early variants' 'stepped' cockpit.

Above: Little is known about the circumstances of where and when this He 111E was photographed.

Opposite top and bottom: This He 111J of *Gross Kampffliegerschule* 5, a bomber training unit was based at Parow in eastern Germany, suffered engine failure on 7 June 1942. With the *werke nummer* 5057, it crash-landed at Bamberg. The J variant was designed following a *Kriegsmarine* requirement for a torpedo and mine-carrying version of the He 111. When the project was dropped by the *Kriegsmarine*, the RLM opted to continue production, though the He 111J mainly served in training schools until it was withdrawn in 1944.

Opposite top: This particular aircraft is thought to be a He 111J which was flown by *Flugzeugführerschule* C 8. Based at Wiener-Neustadt, Eisenstadt, Parndorf and Trausdorf, this flying school closed in June 1944. The aircraft carries factory codes and, on the nose, the school's badge of a three leaf clover.

Opposite bottom: An early example of a He 111P photographed before the war whilst being operated by II/*KG* 53. Note the over-sized wing crosses and that the fact that the aircraft's code is carried not only on the fuselage but upper wing surfaces. The P-variant is of note for it was the first production model to incorporate the characteristic smooth cockpit design that is more commonly associated with the He 111.

This roomier and more aerodynamic glazed cockpit section, which replaced the 'stepped' examples on the earlier variants, was first tested on the He 111V8 in January 1938. The new cockpit design introduced on the He 111P, that housed the nose gunner forward with, above and just behind him, the pilot and the observer, included an asymmetric mounting for an MG 15 machine-gun.

Below: Another pre-war He 111P pictured in its hangar. This aircraft, 56+A66, belonged to *KG* 155 which was re-designated *KG* 55 on 1 May 1939. *KG* 55's first *Geschwaderkommodore* was *Generalmajor* Wilhelm Süssmann, who held the post from March 1937 until March 1940.

Above: A He 111P of 1/*KG* 255 clearing displaying the unit's distinctive emblem of a pink alpine rose with a green stem on a light blue shield. Like *KG* 155, *KG* 255 was re-designated to become part of *KG* 51, also on 1 May 1939. The unit spent most of the summer of 1939 training and recruiting personnel from the various Luftwaffe flight schools.

Opposite top: The German invasion of Poland, the implementation of *Fall Weiss* (literally Case White) which precipitated the Second World War, began on 1 September 1939. Having assigned two airfleets to the campaign – *Luftflotte* 1 (equipped with 807 aircraft and which was augmented by ninety-two seaplanes of *Fliegerfuhrer der Seeluftstreitkrafte*) and *Luftflotte* 4 (627 aircraft, augmented by thirty Slovak aircraft) – the *Luftwaffe* begun the invasion by bombing the undefended civilian town of Wieluń.

The Luftwaffe had in the region of 810 He 111s, of differing variants, when war was declared in September 1939. This number comprised 400 He 111Hs, 349 He 111Ps, forty He 111Es and twenty-one He 111Js. Of these, it is believed that nearly 100 aircraft had been declared unserviceable, which in effect meant that the total Heinkel He 111 strength was just over 700 aircraft.

This picture shows a He 111 H of 3/*KG* 4 being loaded with 50kg bombs at Langenau (Breslau) for operations over Poland, September 1939. Note the open bombs doors, the bombs themselves being stored vertically in the bomb bay. The spinner colours are yellow which indicates that this is a 3 Staffel aircraft. This particular He 111 was commanded by *Oberleutnant* Friedrich-Wilhelm Koch who would be captured 1 July 1940 when he and his crew were shot down over the North Sea by Spitfires of 72 Squadron.

Below: A nose gunner of a Heinkel He 111 pictured whilst his aircraft passes low over a Polish community during the invasion of Poland. The fact that this individual is wearing his forage cap suggests that this may not have been an operational sortie but a flight arranged for obtaining propaganda images.

Left: At the start of the war, some German bombers were allowed to carry unusual personal markings. This is a He 111 P-2, *werke nummer* 2145. of 3/*KG* 55 pictured in September 1939. It was still being operated by this *Kampfgeschwader* in June 1941 as it was recorded as being damaged in combat whilst flown by a 7/*KG* 55 crew on 22 June 1941. *Gefrieter* Karl Kappeler, the *Beobachter*, was wounded. This He 111 was eventually destroyed in an accident on 25 November 1942, whilst with *Flugzeugführerschule* C13, when it crashed at Brunau, injuring three of the men on board.

Below: He 111Ps of I/*KG* 1. The crews of I/*KG* 1 flew from Kolberg during the Polish Campaign. Unusually, I/*KG* 1 retained the codes of its predecessor unit, IV/*KG* 152, hence we know that the farther of these two aircraft, V4+AU, is 1/*KG* 1. This unit retained these codes until March 1941 when it was re-designated III/*KG* 40 and began operating over the Atlantic.

Gefrieter Walter Schwinn, a Bordschütz with 3/*KG* 55, puts the finishing touches to another caricature. Schwinn would be shot down and captured during operations over Belgium on 27 May 1940. As for the He 111 seen here, a P-2 variant with the *werke nummer* 2149, it became coded G1+JA and was reported missing on a reconnaissance flight in the vicinity of Winniza in the Soviet Union on 11 July 1941. The crew at the time, *Leutnant* Karl Doppelhammer (pilot), *Feldwebel* Fritz Bräunig (Beobachter), *Feldwebel* Norbert Schulte (Bordfunker), *Gefrieter* Max Wied (Bordmechaniker), and *Gefrieter* Anton Munster (Bordschütz), were all lost.

Opposite top and bottom: One of the first German losses of the Polish Campaign. This He 111P-2 of 1/*KG* 4, *werke nummer* 1575 and coded 5J+GH, was shot down by *Plutonowy* (Sergeant) Władysław Majchrzyk and *Plutonowy* Antoni Markiewicz of 122 Eskadra Myśliwska (EM – or fighter squadron) on 3 September 1939. *Gefrieter* Walter Dymek managed to crash-land at Golchowice at 08.30 hours. Whilst he and *Obergefreiter* Paul Kania (Bordmechaniker) managed to evade capture, *Unteroffizier* Walter Pfeiffer (Beobachter) and *Gefrieter* Heinz Haibach (Bordfunker) were both killed.

This page: Another early Luftwaffe loss was the He 111P-2 seen here. A 3/*KG* 4 aircraft coded 5J+CL, it was shot down by *Plutonowy* Franciszek Pretkiewicz of 161 EM and *Kapral* Zbigniew Urbanczyk of 162 EM on 6 September 1939.

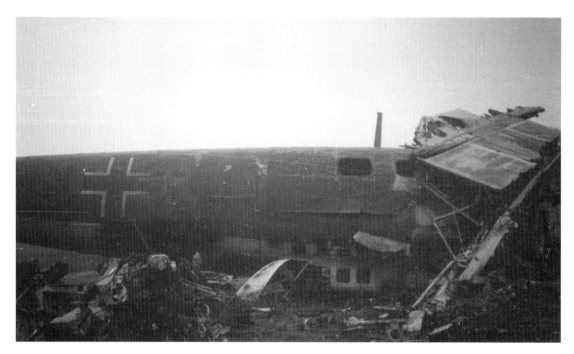

This page: Two further views of the wreckage of 5J+CL after it was shot down and crashed north-west of Grojek at 09.30 hours on 6 September 1939. The crew, *Unteroffizier* Willi Schuy (pilot), *Unteroffizier* Kurt Ambrosius (Beobachter), *Unteroffizier* Johann Seiler (Bordfunker) and *Gefrieter* Raimund Riedel (Bordmechaniker), were all killed.

Above: Coded G1+CL, this He 111P of 3/*KG* 55 is pictured delivering its deadly cargo whilst being flown by *Feldwebel* Heinrich Schmidt. Having undertaken numerous sorties during the invasion of Poland, it would be shot down over Belgium on 27 May 1940 during its eleventh mission in that Blitzkrieg campaign.

Above: Officers of I/KG 55 in front of the tail section of He 111P G1+CL during the Polish Campaign. Left to right are an unnamed officer, *Leutnant* Fritz Schmidtmann (3/KG 55, awarded the Ritterkreuz on 29 February 1944), *Major* Walter Marienfeld (*Gruppen Kommandeur* I/KG 55, awarded the Ritterkreuz on 27 November 1941, killed on 23 October 1944), *Oberleutnant* Heinz Rosenthal (Staffel

Kapitän 3/*KG* 55, killed 3 February 1940 as *Gruppen Kommandeur* I/*KG* 30), *Leutnant* Adalbert Karbe (3/*KG* 55, Ritterkreuz awarded on 12 November 1941, killed on 31 July 1942 whilst serving with IV/*KG* 55).

Below: The 4T markings underneath the wing of this snow-covered He 111 identify the unit as Wettererkundungsstaffel 51. Wettererkundungsstaffeln (also known as Wekusta or Westa) were Luftwaffe flying units of squadron strength used for weather reconnaissance. Their primary task was to collect weather data in areas that only aircraft could penetrate.

Wettererkundungsstaffel 51, more commonly known as Wekusta 51, was formed at Roth in June 1939 and remained there until after the Battle of France. The unit was commanded by *Oberleutnant* Gerd Nissen who was captured on 12 June 1940 when his He 111 was shot down off the Thames Estuary by Spitfires of 64 and 610 squadrons. *Oberfeldwebel* Hans Peckhaus was also captured, but Weather Forecaster Dr Hermann Freudenberg, *Unteroffizier* Franz Boinski and *Unteroffizier* Willi Stiegelmeier were killed.

Above; During the Second World War around 1,200 enemy aircraft were brought down over the British Isles. The Heinkel seen here, lying on moorland at Long Newton Farm near the hamlet of Humbie on the Lammermuir Hills in southern Scotland. The wreckage is that of of *Leutnant* Rolf Niehoff's Heinkel He 111H-2, which, in turn, was the first enemy aircraft to fall on the British mainland since 1918, pictured near the hamlet of Humbie

Despite the fact that the war was less than two months old, *Luftwaffe* raiders had already operated against targets in and around Scotland and the very north of England with 602 and 603 squadrons claiming victories over the North Sea against Junkers Ju 88s and a Heinkel He 111 on 16 and 22 October respectively. Operating at long range over the North Sea, the German raids were clearly

risky. Conducted during daylight hours, and with no possibility of any fighter cover, the raiders were flying into a sensitive and well-defended area. With the strategically important naval base at Scapa Flow and the shipyards and docks of Greenock off to the west, the region was patrolled almost constantly by sections of the various squadrons of Fighter Command's 13 Group.

It was into this area that *Leutnant* Rolf Niehoff, as captain of the Heinkel He 111H-2 coded 1H+JA (*werke nummer* 5449), brought his Stab/*KG* 26 crew on that fateful morning of 28 October 1939. Whilst Niehoff (who was the Beobachter) and *Unteroffizier* Kurt Lehmkuhl (pilot) were both captured, *Gefrieter* Bruno Reimann (Bordfunker) and *Unteroffizier* Gottlieb Kowalke (Bordmechaniker) were both killed.

Above: Another view of the wreckage of *Leutnant* Niehoff's He 111. This is in fact a still taken from wartime news footage. Niehoff later recalled the events of 28 October 1939 thus:

'When we returned from the area of Glasgow, flying at a height of about 12,000 to 15,00ft we were greeted by anti-aircraft fire. One shot must have been a hit because I heard the explosion and felt the impact, but I do not think much damage was done … A short time after the anti-aircraft fire four Spitfires appeared and began attacking, one after the other. My two rear gunners were, of course, at their weapons and alert. They were *Gefrieter* Bruno Reimann and *Unteroffizier* Gottlieb Kowalke. Twice before we had had contact with enemy fighters but this time my gunners started shooting back far too early, so that the first Spitfire killed them both as they were changing their spent ammunition

drums. Before I could go to look after my gunners, my young but very able pilot, *Unteroffizier* Kurt Lehmkuhl, was hit in the back by two bullets and I had to stay with him in the cockpit in case he fainted.

'Now, of course, the Spitfires got no more machine-gun fire from our aircraft and they flew very close to our rear. Therefore, most of their bullets hit our wings and engines which soon stopped. Only a few more bullets hit the cockpit, which is why I and my pilot survived. The four Spitfires were shooting at us, one after the other, right up until we hit the ground.'

Opposite top: Civilians and service personnel alike examine the remains of Niehoff's Heinkel near Humbie. It has been established that this aircraft was manufactured at the Heinkel-Werke factory in Oranienburg during October 1938.

To this day debate continues as to which squadron or pilot was the victor over 1H+JA. Post–war research, however, has credited the victory to Flight Lieutenant Archibald 'Archie' McKellar. A pilot with Red Section, 'A' Flight, 602 (City of Glasgow) Squadron, McKellar later described the events that day in his combat report:

'Patrolling T'house 16,000ft noticed AA fire N of my position. Saw 1 a/c heading S.E. at 14,000ft approx. Being doubtful of identity asked T'house for information. Put section into line astern full boost & followed. Identified as hostile. Carried out No.2 attack, my No.2 followed with No.1 attack. E/A dodged into cloud & I followed him. He appeared again when I & No.2 attacked. Noticed port engine disabled with smoke issuing. Machine started to circle. Reported to T'house E/A appeared to be going down. Three other Spitfires then came in and attacked. Saw machine land approx. 6 miles due south of Tranent.'

Below: A close up of the 'Vestigium Leonis' emblem of *KG* 26 on the Humbie Heinkel.

Opposite top: Five days after the shooting down of the Humbie Heinkel, He 111H-2 *werke nummer* 5350 and coded F6+EK, of 2(F)/122, was intercepted by Flight Lieutenant Robert Voase Jeff of 87 Squadron over northern France. Badly damaged, the bomber force-landed at Staple near Hazebrouck. *Feldwebel* Werner Schmidt (pilot), *Oberleutnant* Wilhelm Ohmsen (Beobachter) and *Unteroffizier* Wilhelm Jung (Bordfunker) were all captured; *Unteroffizier* Franz Wezel (Bordmechaniker) was mortally wounded.

This kill was the first recorded victory for the RAF's Advanced Air Striking Force. For his actions, Jeff was awarded the *Croix de Guerre* – it is stated that he was 'the first British officer to receive a French award in the present war'. He would survive the Battle of France with four confirmed and one unconfirmed kills only to be reported missing in action off Portland Bill in Dorset on 11 August 1940.

Opposite bottom: This is believed to be a picture showing the wreckage of Flight Lieutenant Robert Voase Jeff's victim, He 111H-2 *werke nummer* 5350 and coded F6+EK, being transported away by the French military.

Below: A number of Heinkel He 111s pictured, almost certainly at Nordhausen, during the winter of 1939-40. The aircraft nearest appears to be a He 111P of *KG* 1. It carries an unidentified white emblem on the nose.

Above and below: Another Heinkel casualty from the winter of 1939-40 – though the circumstances of this incident are unknown. The code letters A1+BT tells us that this aircraft is from 9/*KG* 53. III/*KG* 53 did not take part in the Polish Campaign but remained in training at Giebelstadt and Schwäbisch Hall until the start of the Battle of France, carrying out the occasional leaflet raid during the Phoney War.

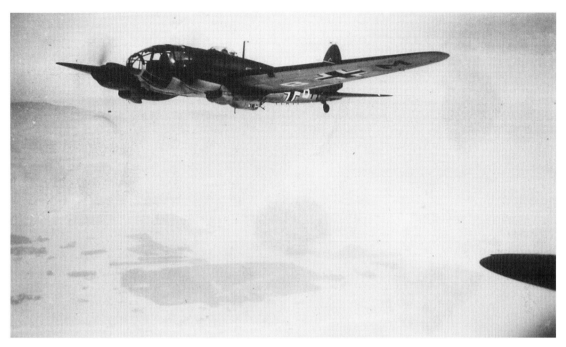

This page: Two air-to-air shots depicting aircraft from 4/*KG* 28. This unit was formed from II/*KG* 254 in May 1939. The pictures themselves were taken between 8 January and 24 April 1940 when the unit was based at Marienburg having been re-designated II/*KG* 54 in December 1939 and then reformed later that same month. It would appear that its He 111s were returned to Heinkel at Rostock at the end of April 1940 after which it was again disbanded.

Above: Another Heinkel from 4/*KG* 28, in this case one that is coded 2F+FM.

Below: The code letters 1H+BB on this He 111 identify it as being from Stab I/*KG* 26. >>

1940. KG *26* was actively involved in missions against shipping in the North Sea or targets along the British coastline for the first seven months of the war.

Left: Another example of the 'Vestigium Leonis' emblem on the side of a He 111 of *KG 26*. The colours used on this badge varied depending on the Gruppe involved. For example, I Gruppe was represented by a black lion on a white shield, whilst II Gruppe was a red lion on a white shield. For its part, III Gruppe aircraft carried a black lion on a yellow shield. The Stab of each of these Gruppen had green shields with a white lion for Stab I, red lion for Stab II and a yellow lion for Stab III.

Below: A Heinkel He 111H of a 2 Staffel pictured in the snow. Possibly a *KG* 55 aircraft photographed early in 1940, it was coded EK (the letters being in red) and had red spinners.

The photograph was probably taken at Lübeck-Blankensee or Westerland Sylt in early

This page and opposite: This series of four photographs detail the end result of an apparently inconclusive, to the RAF at least, Phoney War combat. At 09.45 hours on 29 January 1940, Hurricanes of 43 Squadron intercepted a He 111H-3 of 2/*KG* 26 (2 Staffel was commanded by *Hauptmann* Hans-Joachim Helm) off Hartlepool.

After a brief combat, the RAF fighters broke away. With no evidence of the bomber being shot down or fatally damaged, the Hurricane pilots did not file any claims. As this series of images reveal, however, it would appear that the German bomber had been damaged and limped back on one engine, eventually crash-landing on the German coast. There were no casualties on either side.

Above: The first German aircraft to fall on English soil in the Second World War was the He 111H-2 seen here (a Heinkel He 115 brought down at Sheringham, Norfolk, on 6 December 1939 is generally described as having fallen in the sea). Coded 1H+FM and with the *werke nummer* 2323, it was operated by 4/*KG* 26 – 4 Staffel was commanded by *Hauptmann* Eberhard Schnor von Carolsfeld.

Opposite top: Having taken off from Schleswig on the morning of Staurday, 3 February 1940 for an armed reconnaissance off the British Coast, 1H+FM was intercepted by Hurricanes of 43 Squadron. The victorious fighters were those flown by Flight Lieutenant Peter Townsend, Flying Officer Pat Folkes and Sergeant Jim Hallowes.

Opposite bottom: Flown by *Feldwebel* Hermann Wilms, 1H+FM was crash-landed at Bannial Flat Farm, Sneaton near Whitby in Yorkshire at 09.40 hours. Wilms and *Unteroffizier* Karl Missy (Bordfunker) were captured, though wounded, whilst *Unteroffizier* Rudolf Leushacke (Beobachter) and *Unteroffizier* Johann Meyer (Bordmechaniker) were both killed. Missy's injuries were so severe, having lost his right leg, that he was repatriated to Germany in October 1943 during a prisoner of war exchange.

Opposite top: The extent of the damage caused to 1H+FM during the crash-landing is evident in this image. Two other *KG* 26 He 111s were lost on the morning of 3 February 1940 – one apiece from 2/*KG* 26 and 3/*KG* 26 (these being 1H+GK and 1H+HL respectively). Both bombers, further victims of the Hurricanes of 43 Squadron, fell into the icy waters of the North Sea.

Opposite bottom: Despite its broken back, amongst other damage, *Leutnant* Rolf Niehoff's Heinkel He 111H-2 which crashed at Humbie was still of considerable value in terms of a technical evaluation by the RAF. It could not, however, be made airworthy for flight testing. That opportunity was presented to the British authorities on 9 February 1940, when another He 111 of *KG* 26, coded 1H+EN, came down not that far from Humbie in a field at North Berwick Law in East Lothian – as seen here.

Top right: This aircraft, 1H+EN of 5/*KG* 26 (5 Staffel was commanded by *Oberleutnant* Sighard Dommer), was shot down whilst engaged on an armed shipping reconnaissance flight, also in the Firth of Forth area. With the *werke nummer* 6853, 1H+EN had taken off from Westerland-Sylt with *Unteroffizier* Helmut Meyer at the controls.

Right: The interception of 1H+EN was undertaken by Squadron Leader Andrew Farquhar and Flying Officer A.M. Grant of 602 Squadron. The other crew members on board with Meyer were *Unteroffizier* Josef Sangl (Beobachter) and *Obergefreiter* Heinz Hegemann (Bordmechaniker) and *Unteroffizier* Franz Wieners (Bordfunker). They were all captured, with the exception of Wieners who was killed in the engagement.

Opposite: Although damaged, as the images on the previous pages clearly illustrate, 1H+EN was deemed repairable, the initial work being carried out on site. The bomber was then moved to RAF Turnhouse near Edinburgh, following which it was flown to the Royal Aircraft Establishment at Farnborough for detailed examination, being allotted the serial AW177.

Above: AW177 was the first enemy aircraft to arrive in Britain that would subsequently be test flown. In September 1941 it was transferred to the Air Fighting Development Unit at RAF Duxford and then, in December 1941, to No.1426 (Enemy Aircraft) Flight. Nicknamed 'the Rafwaffe', No.1426 (Enemy Aircraft) Flight was formed to evaluate captured enemy aircraft and demonstrate their characteristics to other Allied units.

Above: On 10 November 1943, while landing at Polebrook airfield in Northamptonshire, home of the US 351st Bomb Group, AW177 and a captured Junkers Ju 88, which had been allotted the serial number HM509, used the same runway simultaneously from opposite ends. Although they did not collide, Flying Officer F.A. 'Freddie' Barr opened the Heinkel's throttles, did a steep turn, stalled and spun in vertically just outside the airfield perimeter killing himself and six of the ten passengers.

Opposite: An interior view showing the gunners' positions on a He 111.

Above; The calm before the storm. He 111s of 7/*KG* 54, those in the foreground being coded B3+JR and B3+BR, seen at Celle in Germany in April 1940. III/*KG* 54 was not formed until February 1940 and 7/*KG* 54 would be commanded by *Hauptmann* Jobst Heinrich von Heydebreck until the end of June 1940. *KG* 54 would play a big part in the Battle of France after which it would convert to the Junkers Ju 88 and be similarly involved in the Battle of Britain. Interestingly, these aircraft do not carry the 'Totenkopf' skull badge of KG *54* below the cockpit.

Below: Another unit which would convert to the Junkers Ju 88 having been actively involved in the Battle of France was *KG* 51. This aircraft is from 8/*KG* 51, which was commanded by *Hauptmann* Gundolf Von Schenk. Note the small crosses underneath the wingtips. The spinners would have been in red.

Below: On the evening of 30 April 1940, HMS *Golden Eagle*, an Auxiliary Anti-Aircraft Vessel, was steaming along fixed patrol lines in the Thames Estuary. As midnight approached, the sound of an enemy aircraft could be heard. Moments later, the guns on *Golden Eagle* went into action.

The aircraft that had been detected by HMS *Golden Eagle* was the Heinkel He 111H-4 of 3/*Kampfgruppe* 126, coded 1T+EL, flown by *Oberleutnant* Hermann Vagts. The German crew's mission that night was to undertake mine-laying along the Norfolk/Suffolk coast. As the bomber approached the East Coast, it encountered a thick blanket of fog out at sea.

Losing track of their position, Vagts and his crew of *Leutnant* Hermann Wilhelm Sodtmann (Beobachter), *Unteroffizier* Hans-Günter Koch (Bordfunker) and *Unteroffizier* Karl-Heinz (Bordmechaniker), found themselves picked up by the Chain Home radar station at Bawdsey.

It was at about this time that the first anti-aircraft fire targeted the lone intruder; not only did HMS *Golden Eagle* unleash its barrage, so did shore batteries at Felixstowe and Harwich.

Hit and losing height, Vagts circled the coastal resort of Clacton-on-Sea. Just before midnight the bomber crashed amongst residential properties in and around Victoria Road. This view of the wreckage of the Heinkel was taken looking north up Upper Victoria Road. The house in the background is No.33.

Above: Soon after 1T+EL slammed into the ground, the crash site was devastated by a huge explosion; both the aircraft and one of the 1,000kg Luftmine B parachute mines (referred to by the British as the Admiralty Type C) it had been carrying ignited with a deafening blast.

One of Clacton's Air Raid Wardens, Mr A. Knight, had come out from his nearby home to investigate. 'I was reading in bed when I heard the noise of the airplane coming down,' he recalled. 'I ran out in my dressing gown and saw the airplane and the house burning. As I got within thirty yards the whole thing went up. Luckily I flung myself on the ground just in time. I hurt my knee and got hit by a certain amount of flying debris, but no serious damage was done. My ear drums were so

affected that I could not hear from some hours afterwards.'

A total of 156 people were injured during the crash and subsequent explosion, thirty-four of whom were described as 'serious' and required hospitalisation. Two people, Fredrick and Dorothy Gill, were killed when their home, No.25 Upper Victoria Road, virtually disintegrated. They were the first civilian deaths of the war in England to have resulted from enemy action.

Vagts and his three colleagues in 1T+EL's crew were killed. It is the body of one of these men seen here being removed from the crash site.

Above: Another unit which would have an active part to play in the invasion of Norway and Battle of Britain was the pathfinder unit *Kampfgruppe* 100. Equipped with X Gerät bombing aid (the fitting of which was always distinguished by three aerial masts on the fuselage), this He 111H-1 of 2/*Kampfgruppe* 100 (commanded by *Oberleutnant* Gerd Korthals) was photographed at Köthen in the spring of 1940.

The X-Gerät, or X-Apparatus, used a series of beams to locate the target, each beam being named after a river. The previous system used by the Luftwaffe, which was called Knickebein, was never intended to be utilised in the long-range role. Efforts to produce a much more accurate version of the same basic concept eventually resulted in the X-Gerät system. Accuracy of X-Gerät was considerably better than Knickebein, but as it operated on completely different frequencies it required new radio equipment to be used. There was not nearly enough to go around, so instead the experimental unit *Kampfgruppe* 100 was given the task of using their sets in order to guide other planes to the target. To do this *Kampfgruppe* 100 aircraft would attack as a small group first, dropping flares which other planes would then see and bomb visually. This is the first use of the pathfinder concept that the RAF would later use to great effect against the Germans only a few years later.

Above: Another blind bombing aid which was being developed early on in the war was Y Verfähren, the fitment of its equipment being indicated by a single larger aerial just behind the cockpit. The aircraft seen here, and fitted with the tell-tale Y Verfähren aerial, is a He 111H-5 of Eprobungestelle Rechlin and was attached to *Kampfgruppe* 100 for proving trials in the summer of 1940. III/*KG* 26 would be the only unit to use Y Verfähren in the Blitz.

The Y Verfähren, literally Y System, used a single narrow beam pointed over the target, transmitting a modulated radio signal. The system utilised a new piece of equipment that received the signal from the beam and immediately re-transmitted it back to the ground station. The ground station listened for the return signal and compared the phase of its modulation to the transmitted signal. This was an accurate way of measuring the transit time of the signal, and hence the distance to the aircraft. Coupled with the direction of the beam (adjusted for a maximum return signal), the bomber's position could be established with considerable accuracy. The bombers did not have to track the beam, instead the ground controllers could calculate it and then give radio instructions to the pilot to correct the flight path.

Opposite top and bottom: A He 111 of Wekusta 51 which has suffered what appears to be a double engine failure. The airfield is believed to be Roth, though the exact date of the incident is unknown.

Above: Coded 6N+GL, this He 111H of 3/*Kampfgruppe* 100 is seen here at Lüneberg during the spring of 1940. Note the aircraft letter 'G' on the leading edge of the wing and the characteristic Viking long boat emblem carried by all Kampfgruppe 100 aircraft. The boat in the badge was black, shields white, sail red and white, pennant red, and the waves white – all on a blue disc. The letter 'G' and spinners would have been coloured yellow.

Right: An unidentified crew of *KG* 26 seen just prior to the Norwegian Campaign. All but the officer in the centre are sensibly wearing winter flying suits.

Above: A Heinkel He 111H of *Kampfgruppe 100*, in this case coded 6N+DK, is pictured taking off from Nordholz on 9 April 1940 – the date that German forces commenced Operation *Weserübung*, the invasion of Norway and Denmark. The crew of 6N+DK was en route to Oslo, its specific target being the Oscarsborg Fortress, a system of coastal defences in the Oslofjord, close to the small town of Drøbak.

The Luftwaffe force successfully attacked the fortress, but not before the Norwegian defenders had sunk the German heavy cruiser *Blücher*. Despite the fact that the fortress' armament was over forty years old, both the guns and the torpedo battery worked flawlessly when it engaged one of the German invasion flotillas. In what has become known as the Battle of Drøbak Sound, *Blücher* was sunk, disrupting the Kriegsmarine force heading for Oslo, thus managing to save the Norwegian King and government from being taken prisoner.

The Luftwaffe attacks on Oscarsborg Fortress were carried in a series of waves. In all, the fortress was subjected to nearly nine hours of aerial bombardment, during which around 500 bombs, ranging from 50kg to 200 kg in size, were dropped.

Above: A dramatic shot of Heinkel He 111Hs of *Kampfgruppe* 100 over the Skaggerak on 9 April 1940. Not all of the aircraft have the three aerials showing they are fitted with X Gerät, whilst on the nearest bomber can again be seen *Kampfgruppe* 100's Viking emblem.

Opposite page: These two pictures show the aftermath of one sortie over Norway during Operation *Weserübung*. This He 111H, coded 6N+AK, was that of *Oberleutnant* Gerd Korthals, the Staffel Kapitän of 2/*Kampfgruppe* 100, was hit by anti-aircraft fire.

Above and below: Accidents happen. It would appear that 6N+KK's port wingtip has connected with the tail of another 2/*Kampfgruppe* 100 He 111H. Note that in both cases the aircraft letter is now red.

It is believed this accident occurred at Trondheim on 3 May 1940. Norway's second city and the strategic key to the whole country, Trondheim had fallen to the Germans in the earliest stages of Operation *Weserübung*.

Above: Hauptmann Artur von Casimir, seen here on top of the cockpit of a *Kampfgruppe* 100 Heinkel He 111, became the *Gruppen Kommandeur* of the unit following the death of *Oberstleutnant* Joachim Stollbrock. The latter was shot down by Spitfires of 54 Squadron over the Thames Estuary at 17.00 hours on 13 February 1940.

The aircraft in this picture is believed to be the He 111H-3, coded 6N+AB, in which von Casimir was in turn shot down on 29 May 1940. The victor on this occasion was 24-year-old Flying Officer Jack Wykeham Lydall who had been at the controls of a 46 Squadron Hurricane, L1816. Von Casimir had taken off from Trondheim to attack British shipping at Ofotfjorden near Narvik. Following the

combat with Lydall, he force-landed at Ulsvåg in the province of Hamarøy, Norway. Both he and *Oberleutnant* Wolfgang Metzke were captured and spent most of the war in Canada. The Bordmechaniker, *Unteroffizier* Walter Schwarz, was killed, whilst Helmut Grubbe (Beobachter) and *Unteroffizier* Ewald Korth (Bordfunker) were both wounded, captured and later released. The number '52' that can be seen just in front of the *Kampfgruppe* 100 emblem represents the last two digits of the *werke nummer*.

Flight Officer Lydall was shot down and killed near Beisjford later on the same day. He is buried in Narvik New Cemetery.

Above: *Kampfgruppe* 100 briefly operated
from the frozen Lake Jonsvatnet near
Trondheim during the early stages of the
Norwegian Campaign. The individual in the
centre of the small group man-handling the
oil drum has been identified as
Oberfeldwebel Hilmar Schmidt, a Beobachter
with 2/*Kampfgruppe* 100. The aircraft behind
the three men is 6N+OH of 1/*Kampfgruppe*
100. Schmidt and his crew first arrived at
Trondheim on 16 April 1940, when this
photograph is believed to have been taken,
but left the next day.

Above: Personnel of *Kampfgruppe* 100 on the frozen Lake Jonsvatnet airfield in April 1940. The person on the left, seen here in discussion with unidentified crews from 1/*Kampfgruppe* 100, is *Oberleutnant* Gerd Korthals. Immediately behind him is the tail of a 2/*Kampfgruppe* 100 He 111 (probably a H-1 or H-2 variant) which appears to have the

werke nummer 3093. In the background is 6N+FH of 1/*Kampfgruppe* 100.

Below: Heinkel He 111s of *Kampfgruppe* 100 dispersed on the ice of Lake Jonsvatnet. The nearest, a H-3 coded 6N+AB, is the aircraft flown by *Hauptmann* Artur Von Casimir when he was shot down on 29 May 1940.

Opposite top: Although poor quality, this image shows a He 111H-1, *werke nummer* 2320 and coded 6N+NH, of 1/*KG* 100. On 20 April 1940, this particular aircraft was being flown by *Hauptmann* Artur von Casimir in an attack on Namsos during which it was damaged and he force-landed on the frozen Lake Jonsvatnet. The aircraft eventually sank into the lake when the ice subsequently melted.

Surprisingly, 6N+NH has survived. Recovered and brought back to the surface in September 2004, it is now on display in the Deutsches Technikmuseum in Berlin.

Opposite bottom: After the snow has gone, *Kampfgruppe* 100 rests at Trondheim-Vaernes. Amongst the unit's successes during the Norwegian Campaign were the sinking of the Polish destroyer *Grom*, by *Oberleutnant* Gerd Korthals on 4 May 1940, and the C-class light cruiser HMS *Curlew*, by *Oberfeldwebel*

Wierbitzky, on 26 May 1940.

It was on 4 May 1940, that *Grom* undertook what turned out to be the last of its many naval missions in the Narvik area – more specifically in the Rombaken fjord. Attacked by Korthals' crew, the destroyer's loaded midship torpedo launcher was hit by a bomb and the torpedo exploded, causing the hull to break into two and the ship to sink almost immediately with a loss of life of fifty-nine of the crew. HMS *Curlew* was also attacked and sunk in the Narvik area, more specifically in Lavangsfjord.

The crew of *Oberfeldwebel* Paul Wierbitzky of 2/*Kampfgruppe* 100 eventually left Trondheim on 8 June 1940 in preparation for operations against mainland Britain.

Above: Heinkel He 111s of *Kampfgruppe* 100 pictured in formation over Norway during the spring of 1940. The three X Gerät aerials make aircraft of this unit easily recognisable.

Above: This He 111 from 3/*KG* 4 was damaged by anti-aircraft fire over Norway during the spring of 1940. It carries the *KG* 4 badge which, white on red, was taken from the family coat of arms of General Walter Wever, *KG* 4 being granted the name 'General Wever'. During the Norwegian Campaign, *KG* 4 operated from Perleberg, Aalborg-West, Kastrup and Oslo Fornebu.

Opposite top: Another unit operating He 111s over Norway was 4/Lehrgeschwader 1. On 25 April 1940, one of this unit's He 111H-3s, that coded L1+KM, was shot down by Gloster Gladiators of 263 Squadron – the latter had only just arrived in theatre and were operating from an improvised air strip on the

frozen Lake Lesjaskogsvatnet in central southern Norway.

L1+KM had taken off from Schleswig at 08.30 hours to attack the British cruisers HMS *Carlisle* and HMS *Curacao* and was intercepted and damaged after it had dropped its bombs. The pilot, *Unteroffizier* Helmut Nolte, managed to land in a snow-covered field at Fiva near Romdahl, only for his aircraft to then skid into the icy River Rauma – where this photograph was taken. Nolte, *Gefrieter* Herbert Schmidt (Beobachter) and *Unteroffizier* Harry Friedrichs (Bordmechaniker) were all captured, whilst *Unteroffizier* Hans Schrader (Bordfunker) was mortally wounded during the combat.

Left: Another Luftwaffe unit to see be deployed over Norway was 8/*KG* 26. On 7 June 1940, *Leutnant* Hermann Riedel was intercepted over Narvik by Hurricanes of 46 Squadron, but managed to return to Trondheim-Vaernes. Safely back on the ground, it was discovered that his He 111, which was coded 1H+LS, had been hit no less than 368 times! The only casualty was gunner *Unteroffizier* Gerhard Markuse who was wounded. The men in this picture are *Oberfeldwebel* Karl Müller (left), *Oberfeldwebel* Paul Süssenbach (middle), and *Gefrieter* Willi Schöll.

Above: The tail of 1H+LS with, to the left, *Gefrieter* Willi Schöll (Beobachter), who was a member of *Leutnant* Hermann Riedel's crew. Schöll was the only member of his crew who did not survive the war. Having been commissioned, and awarded the Ehrenpokal, he was lost whilst serving as Staffel Kapitän of 6/*KG* 100 on 20 April 1944; he would be posthumously awarded the Deutsches Kreuz in Gold.

Right: A He 111H of *KG* 26 flying low over the water off Norway. The aircraft appears to be carrying a 500kg bomb externally.

Opposite: Ground crew clearing snow from a He 111 of *KG* 26. The emblem of *KG* 26 is just visible beneath the open window. The bulge for the Lotfe bomb sight can be clearly seen on the underside of the cockpit.

Opposite top: The German armed forces unleashed their Blitzkrieg in the West on 10 May 1940. This He 111H of 3/*LG* 1, coded L1+EL, was shot down at the end of the first day. Tasked to carry out an armed reconnaissance, it was intercepted by Pilot Officer Arthur Eugene Le Breuilly and Pilot Officer C.R. Rowe of 607 Squadron east of Lille, crash-landing at Ormeignes, just over the Franco-Belgium border, at 17.20 hours. *Feldwebel* Walter Hartmann (the pilot), *Feldwebel* Wilhelm Frank (Beobachter) and *Gefreiter* Max Buhler were all captured; *Unteroffizier* Hans Saas (Bordmechaniker) was killed. Note the rarely-seen winged bomb badge of 3/*LG* 1 just in front of the German soldier standing on the wing root. Le Breuilly would be killed in action four days later.

Opposite bottom: This He 111H-2 of 9/*KG* 1, *werke nummer* 5627 and coded V4+ET, had its port engine damaged by Pilot Officer Peter Parrott and Sergeant Ken Townsend of 607 Squadron whilst attacking airfields near Albert on the afternoon of 10 May 1940. *Leutnant* Kurt Neumann succeeded in crash-landing at Saint-Simon–Clastres at 15.00 hours. Along with the rest of his crew, *Feldwebel* Hans Oppermann (Beobachter), *Flieger* Heinrich Pümpel (Bordschütz) and *Flieger* Willi Pfeiffer (Bordmechaniker), Neumann was taken prisoner.

Above: German bombers were instrumental in the success of the Blitzkrieg. Here a He 111 of 3/*KG* 55, that coded G1+KL, drops its bombs on an unidentified target.

Opposite: A Luftwaffe loss during the Battle of France. On the evening of 12 May 1940, a He 111H of 3/*Kampfgruppe* 126, that coded 1T+AL, was shot down by *Groupe de Chasse* III/3 during an armed reconnaissance of South Beveland and the Scheldt Estuary. The bomber crashed at Calfven, between Hoogerheide and Ossendrecht in the Netherlands, at 20.10 hours.

The crew members who were killed in the incident, *Oberleutnant* Friedrich-Wilhelm Sawade (who was the Staffel Kapitän), *Oberfeldwebel* Herbert Klabunde and *Unteroffizier* Jakob Dethlefsen, were initially buried beside the wreckage of their aircraft. *Oberfeldwebel* Herbert Widmeyer, meanwhile, had managed to bale out and was captured badly wounded.

The inscription on the improvised memorial cross reads: 'Here lies the crew of a He 111, three men killed 12 May 1940.'

A second 3/126 He 111 was also shot down by the French fighters that day, crashing at Woensdrecht in the southern Netherlands at around the same time.

Above: An early loss on the morning of 13 May 1940 was this He 111P 2F+FR of 7/*KG* 28. Its crew had been tasked to attack Charleville. It is believed to have been shot down by the Hurricane flown by Squadron Leader James 'Hank' More of 73 Squadron, crashing at 07.15 hours at Beffu, north-east of Grandpré.

Obergefreiter Kurt Funke was the only fatality. The remaining crew members, *Feldwebel* Hans Görke, *Unteroffizier* Otto Schulz, *Unteroffizier* Paul Schönhoff and *Unteroffizier* Alfred Wötzel, were all captured.

On 9 July 1940, III/*KG* 28 was re-designated II/*KG* 76. At the same time, its crews began the process of converting to the Junkers Ju 88.

Above: This He 111P of 5/*KG* 4 was being flown by *Unteroffizier* Fritz Maas (in the centre) when it was hit by flak over Rosendaal, Holland, on the evening of 13 May 1940. With the starboard wing on fire, Maas successfully crash-landed between Zevenbergen and Terheiden at 18.00 hours, the bomber exploding after the crew had got out. Maas, *Gefrieter* Leonard Korfhage (Beobachter), *Unteroffizier* Horst Pieles (Bordfunker) and *Unteroffizier* Kurt Kranisch (Bordmechaniker) were all captured.

Opposite top: An air-to-air shot of *Unteroffizier* Fritz Maas' He 111P, 5J+FN, taken just after its delivery to 5/*KG* 4 when it was still carrying its factory codes. This was the aircraft in which he and his crew were shot down on 13 May 1940.

Opposite bottom: Monday, 13 May 1940 was a day of frantic activity for *KG* 55. It was also costly, with the unit losing six He 111s, whilst a further three returned from sorties having been damaged. This He 111P-2, G1+GA of Stab/*KG* 55, was one of the six losses.

Above: Flown by *Oberleutnant* Dieter Clemm von Hohenberg, G1+GA was engaged on a reconnaissance sortie in the Charleville-Mézières-Ligny areas when it was attacked by Flying Officer Leslie Clisby of 1 Squadron (and possibly by a French Potez 631 of ECMJ 1/16), coming down at Coulommes-les-Marqueny at 06.45 hours. From the series of images seen here, it was obviously the subject of much interest by advancing German soldiers.

Below: As well as von Hohenberg, two other crew members of G1+GA were taken prisoner after the crash on 13 May 1940 – this pair being *Unteroffizier* Hans Ströbl (Bordmechaniker) and *Gefrieter* Oskar Männer (Bordschütz).
Obergefrieter Hans Bell (Bordfunker), however, was mortally wounded during the combat. The remaining crew member, *Feldwebel* Willi Wolter (Beobachter), survived both the combat and subsequent crash, only to be shot and mortally wounded by gendarmes whilst evading capture.

Above and left: Two further images showing the wreckage of G1+GA being inspected by German troops. Note how the swastika on the tail fin has been removed. *Oberleutnant* Dieter Clemm von Hohenberg would return to *KG* 55 after his release from captivity following the Battle of France. He went on to be awarded the Ehrenpokal and Deutsches Kreuz in Gold. He was killed in an accident on 30 June 1944 whilst returning from an operational sortie. At the time, von Hohenberg was serving as Gruppen Kommodore of II/*LG* 1. He would be posthumously promoted to *Major* and awarded the Ritterkreuz.

Below: This He 111P-2 of 8/*KG* 55 fell to the guns of 1 Squadron's Hurricanes, more specifically those flown by Flight Lieutenant Peter Hanks, Flying Officer Lawrie Lorrimer and Pilot Officer George Goodman, on 13 May 1940. Tasked to bomb Allied troop concentrations near Charleville, it crash-landed at Vendresse at 06.30 hours.

Coded G1+HS, this aircraft was flown by *Oberfeldwebel* Bernhard Hickel who, along with *Feldwebel* Max Hausdöfer (Beobachter), was uninjured. The remaining three crew members, *Feldwebel* Willi Herzog (Bordmechaniker), *Gefrieter* Gerhard Andt (Bordfunker) and *Gefrieter* Gustav Bodenhagen (Bordschütz), were all wounded.

Bernhard Hickel continued flying operationally with 8/*KG* 55 and would be commissioned and awarded the Ehrenpokal and Deutsches Kreuz in Gold. Hickel would cheat death twice more in the ten months after the crash seen here. On the first occasion his He 111 burnt out due to the premature ignition of an incendiary bomb on 20 October 1940. The second incident occurred on 14 March 1941 when he was attacked by a night

fighter during a raid on Liverpool in the Blitz, landing his damaged aircraft at Le Bourget with wounded crew members.

Of the RAF pilots involved in the combat on 13 May 1940, Lawrie Lorimer was killed in action the following day, his Hurricane, L1676, being shot by Bf 109s south-west of Rethel. He remains listed as missing in action and is therefore commemorated on the Runnymede Memorial.

Opposite top: A He 111H of 7/*KG* 53. Coded A1+EP, it was photographed at Giebelstadt in the spring of 1940. *Gruppen Kommandeur Major* Edler von Braun is seen inspecting *Leutnant* Ernst Fischbach and his crew. Fischbach and his crew would be shot down and taken prisoner on 30 August 1940.

Opposite bottom: He 111Hs of 2/*KG* 51. By the start of the Battle of France in May 1940 I/*KG* 51 had converted to the Ju 88, as had II/*KG* 51. The crews of III/*KG* 51, however, continued operating the He 111 through to June 1940.

Opposite top: A He 111 of 8/KG 51, coded 9K+ES, overflies a wintery landscape in early spring 1940.

Opposite bottom: Two members of the crew of *Unteroffizier* Vinzenz Schüll (standing in the centre) are photographed with two groundcrew on 10 May 1940. They are in front of their He 111H, which was coded 9K+LS. Four days after this picture was taken, Schüll's aircraft was intercepted over Sainte-Menehould whilst on a mission to bomb the railway station at Revigny. The attackers, Dewoitine D520s of *Groupe de Chasse* I/3, set the bomber's starboard engine on fire, forcing Schüll to crash-land at Hennmont at 13.25 hours. Schüll, *Unteroffizier* Hans Fischer (Beobachter) and *Unteroffizier* Fritz Koch (Bordmechaniker) were captured, whilst *Unteroffizier* Wilhelm Schäkel (Bordfunker) and *Gefrieter* Willi Eckrich (Bordschütz) were killed.

Above: This photograph hides a tragic story. Shot down over Arras, possibly by Flight

Lieutenant Ian Soden of 56 Squadron, this He 111P of 9/KG 54, which was coded B3+JT, belly-landed near Bois de l'Emprunt, on the Lens-Arras road to the north of Vimy, at 16.00 hours on 18 May 1940.

Having survived the initial combat and subsequent landing, all of the bomber's crew were killed in cold blood, either by French troops or civilians. What happened was corroborated by Sergeant John Craig of 111 Squadron, whose Hurricane had crash-landed in an adjacent field at around the same time.

The dead, *Unteroffizier* Otto Ellinghaus (pilot), *Gefrieter* Ernst Reczniczek (Beobachter), *Obergefreiter* Helmut Jentzmik (Bordfunker) and *Gefrieter* Josef Bradack (Bordmechaniker), were buried in shallow graves alongside the bomber. They were subsequently exhumed. One individual was executed by the Germans in 1941 for their part in the incident.

Note the 'Totenkopf' badge of KG 54 behind the cockpit.

Below: A total of three He 111Ps from 6/*KG* 55 were lost during an attack on railway targets west of Fismes on 18 May 1940 – G1+JP, G1+CP and this aircraft, G1+KP. The latter was shot down by *Groupe de Chasse* I/5 and belly-landed at Taizy. *Feldwebel* Josef Blase was captured unhurt, whilst *Hauptmann* Karl-Heinz Schellmann (the Staffel Kapitän), *Oberfeldwebel* Max Basmann, *Feldwebel* Peter Matz and *Oberfeldwebel* Otto Engel were taken prisoner, albeit wounded. Schellmann would eventually command Transportgruppe 30, being reported missing on a sortie to Corsica on 12 November 1943.

Opposite top: The fighting on 19 May 1940 was costly for *KG* 54 which lost no less than thirteen He 111s. This is He 111P-2 *werke nummer* 2673, coded B3+EM, of 4/*KG* 54 which was flown by *Leutnant* Franz

Gottschling. It was shot down by a series of fighters from 85, 87 and 242 squadrons, Gottschling crash-landing at 12.30 hours at Pont-a-Marc, south of Lille.

Opposite bottom: Another view of B3+EM on 19 May 1940. Despite the onslaught of the RAF fighters, Gottschling was captured unwounded, whilst *Gefrieter* Helmut Bönninghaus (Bordmechaniker) was captured wounded. *Oberleutnant* Hermann Sauer (Beobachter) was mortally wounded and *Unteroffizier* Walter Nickel (Bordfunker) killed. Once again, note the 'Totenkopf' emblem behind the cockpit and the diagonal fuselage band which goes through the B3, a marking peculiar to *KG* 54. The aircraft also carried the name *Esel II*. It is known that Gottschling had force-landed another He 111P at Varelbusch on 10 May 1940, possibly *Esel I*.

This page: This He 111 P of an unidentified unit was brought down by RAF fighters during the heavy fighting over the Western Front on 19 May 1940. It is possible that this aircraft is one of the five lost by III/*KG* 27, to 1 Squadron, just before midday.

Above and below: With *Feldwebel* Heinrich
Schmidt at the controls, this He 111P of 3/*KG*
55, which was coded G1+CL, had flown a total
of ten operational sorties during the Battle of
France. However, Schmidt's luck ran on 27 May
1940 when his aircraft was hit by anti-aircraft
fire whilst attacking troop concentrations north
of Ypres in Belgium. He was forced to put his
aircraft down near Langemarck at 11.45 hours.

Schmidt, *Oberfeldwebel* Erich Botzki
(Beobachter), *Unteroffizier* Hans Kaufhold
(Bordfunker), *Unteroffizier* Fritz Wicklein
(Bordmechaniker) and *Gefrieter* Walter
Schwinn (Bordschütz) were all captured and
later released. Both Botzki and Schmidt
would be awarded the Ehrenpokal. With the
rank of *Leutnant*, Schmidt was captured on 26
December 1944 whilst serving with 5/*LG* 1, by
which time he had been awarded the
Deutsches Kreuz in Gold. Kaufhold would be
shot down and captured a second time in
April 1941.

Above: A well-photographed He 111P-2 of 4/*KG* 54. Coded B3+JM and with the *werke nummer* 2585, it was shot down by 92 Squadron early in the morning of 2 June 1940.

Opposite top: After its tangles with one or more of 92 Squadron's Spitfires, B3+JM's pilot, *Oberleutnant* Günther Seubert, belly-landed on the beach at Middelkerke in Belgium at 08.00 hours. Whilst Seubert was unwounded, *Unteroffizier* Hans Bayer (Bordfunker) and *Unteroffizier* Kurt Fiedler (Bordmechaniker) were injured, being treated at a military hospital in Ostend. The other crew member, *Unteroffizier* Franz Härter (Beobachter), was killed.

Opposite bottom: German personnel gather around B3+JM at Middelkerke in the immediate aftermath of the Dunkirk evacuation. As for Seubert, he went on to become the Staffel Kapitän of 4/*KG* 54 on 22 August 1940. He was reported missing during a mission over Russia on 4 March 1942.

Opposite top and bottom: German soldiers could do little to recover B3+JM from its resting place on the beach at Middelkerke and it was soon submerged as the tide came in. Within days, the Heinkel was being broken up by the action of the waves.

Below: As the German forces advanced towards the Channel coast, they would find countless crash-landed bombers. In this photograph, German soldiers inspect a He 111 from *KG* 1 (note the code V4 in the enhanced image on the right, is just visible ahead of the fuselage cross) which has come down near Hazebrouck with at least its port engine stopped.

Above: The *werke nummer* 5654 on the tail of this He 111 identifies it as a H-3 manufactured on behalf of Heinkel by *Allgemeine Transportanlagen-Gesellschaft* in Leipzig. Unfortunately, only the letter G is visible on the fuselage which is not enough to identify the unit. Someone, it would appear, has removed the swastika as a trophy, whilst an attempt may have been made to camouflage the fuselage.

Opposite top and bottom: Two views of another shot-down Heinkel He 111. Apart from the last letter A on the fuselage, which would indicate that this is a Stab aircraft, no other forms of identification are visible.

Above: An exact identification of this He 111P is also not possible, aside from the fact that the distinctive 'Totenkopf' emblem which can be seen behind the cockpit indicates it was operated by *KG* 54.

Opposite top: Another unidentified crash-landing, but this time the unit is *KG* 55, the unit being identified by the Griffon emblem behind the cockpit.

Opposite bottom: Believed to be a He 111H from *KG* 1, this aircraft carries an early fuselage cross and an unidentified badge on the nose, part of which appears to be the outline of Great Britain. This Heinkel appears to have come off the hardstanding and has become bogged down.

Above: Having flown in Poland, Norway, and France, the crews of KG 4 were amongst the first to participate in a major attack on mainland Britain on the night of 18 June 1940. From left to right are: *Oberleutnant* Ernst-Dietrich von Tellemann (Adjutant of II/*KG* 4l; killed on 30 June 1944 whilst Gruppen Kommodore III/*KG* 4); hidden behind von Tellemann is an individual who remains unidentified; *Oberleutnant* Joachim von Arnim (4/*KG* 4, shot down and captured over the UK on 19 June 1940); *Major* Wolfgang Erdmann (Gruppen Kommodore II/*KG* 4, who was awarded the Ritterkreuz and Deutsches Kreuz in Gold); and *Oberleutnant* Ulrich Jordan (Stab II/*KG* 4 – shot down and captured during his first, and last, sortie over the UK on 19 June 1940).

    Major Dietrich Freiherr von Massenbach would take command of II/*KG* 4 in December 1939. He was another member of II/*KG* 4 shot down and captured over the UK on 19 June 1940. He was awarded the Ritterkreuz whilst in captivity.

Opposite top: The code letters 5J+AC on this aircraft indicate that it is from Stab II/*KG* 4 and would normally be the aircraft flown by the *Gruppen Kommandeur*, who was either *Major* Wolfgang Erdmann or *Major* Dietrich Freiherr von Massenbach. Note the individual aircraft letter on top of the wings by the cross.

Opposite bottom: A He 111H of 4/*KG* 4. The officer second from right is *Oberleutnant* Joachim von Arnim who, as we have already seen, became a prisoner of war on 19 June 1940. Note the white spinners and no unit badge. Von Arnim later recalled the operation in which he was shot down:

    'It was a full moon that night and, as far I remember, no clouds whatsoever. Before crossing the coast en route to Mildenhall, we were easily found by searchlights and unable to evade.

    'On approaching our target, the rear gunner [*Feldwebel* Karl] Hauck reported night fighters in sight. They immediately attacked us, hundreds of bullets hit our aircraft from the rear – it sounded like somebody hitting a

thousand drums. Fortunately for us we had installed, just a day before, armour plating in the cockpit and for the two in the rear of the plane. The Spitfire made several attacks on us – it was funny to see the tracer going down in front of us.'

Below: Another unidentified Stab aircraft, the German soldiers blocking any emblem which might help identify the unit. Note the fitment of a beam fuselage gun, this being the result of the need for more defensive armament which in itself necessitated increasing the He 111 crew compliment by one.

Opposite top: This aircraft has been identified as a He 111H-1 of 4/KG 53. Coded A1+AM (though its full identity is not known), it crash-landed at Villingen in Germany. The strange aerials are in fact the chimneys of a factory located beyond the bomber.

Opposite bottom: German soldiers pose for the camera in front of the battered fuselage of an unidentified He 111, the unit emblem being obscured by the open side window. Exactly how this aircraft came to be in the field in this state, with its undercarriage down, is a mystery.

Above: The full *werke nummer* of this He 111P-2 is believed to be 2596, though this is not enough to identify how it was shot down, or indeed when and where.

Right: This scene of destruction, the shattered remains of a shot-down Heinkel He 111, was photographed by advancing German soldiers in the summer of 1940, almost certainly in the Pas de Calais/Dunkirk area.

Above: One of the first Heinkel losses following the Blitzkrieg through the Low Countries and France, this is recorded as being the He 111H-4 of Stab II/*KG* 4, *werke nummer* 8747 and coded 5J+DM, which was shot down at 00.45 hours on 19 June 1940. The victors were two Bristol Blenheims of 23 Squadron, one of which was crewed by Flight Lieutenant Raymond Duke-Wooley and Aircraftman Derek Bell, the other by Sergeant Alan Close and Leading Aircraftman Lawrence Karasek. Close's and Karasek's Blenheim was also shot down and Close killed.

Major Dietrich Freiherr von Massenbach (who was flying as the Beobachter), *Oberleutnant* Ulrich Jordan (pilot), *Oberfeldwebel* Max Leimer (Bordfunker) and *Feldwebel* Karl Amberger (Bordmechaniker) were all captured following their force-landing at Blakeney Creek, Cley, Norfolk.

The code of this aircraft would indicate it was from 4/*KG* 4, von Massenbach no doubt using it as his crew's usual aircraft had been damaged during an air attack on Merville on 14 June 1940.

Above: In the foreground are the burnt out remains of Bristol Blenheim L9477 of 139 Squadron, whilst in the background are He 111s of *KG* 27. Between February and May 1940, 139 Squadron operated out of Plivot as part of the Advanced Air Striking Force. There is no record of L9477 being lost in action.

Below: A selection of Luftwaffe aircraft – a Junkers Ju 87, Heinkel He 111, Junkers Ju 88 and a Messerschmitt Bf 109 – pictured at Brussels during the visit of *Reichsmarschall* Hermann Göring to Luftflotte 2 at some stage during the early days of the Battle of Britain. The identity of the units involved is not known.

Above: Heinkel He 111s of III/*KG* 55 during a
flypast over Paris, the Arc de Triomphe
directly below them. The marks on the
fuselage of the He 111P are thought to
represent the numbers of missions that this
aircraft has flown. III/*KG* 55 was based at
Villacoublay on the outskirts of Paris from 23
June 1940 to 18 June 1941. The griffon
emblem and the toned down camouflage
would indicate that this photograph was
taken during the latter stages of the Battle of
Britain/early stages of the Blitz.

Above: The same two He 111s during their low-level flight. Note the unusual mottled camouflage adopted by III/*KG* 55. The white spinners and the code letter 'F' on the aircraft nearest the camera suggests that this is G1+FR of 7/*KG* 55. During the time this unit was based at Villacoublay it was commanded by *Oberleutnant* Hans Bröcker (killed in action on 25 September 1940), *Oberleutnant* Walter Hesse (prisoner of war on 13 March 1941) and *Oberleutnant* Joachim Herrfurth.

Below: By mid-June 1940, II/KG 4 had arrived at Merville in preparation for its first mission against Great Britain. The He 111 see here is from 6/KG 4. Note the British tin helmet hanging by the tent's opening. On this unit's first mission on the night of 18 June 1940, six He 111s would be lost over the UK, whilst another crash-landed on the beach east of Calais. Six aircrew would be killed, three reported missing and eleven taken prisoner.

Below: A Heinkel He 111H of either I or II/KG 55 which operated out of Dreux and Chartres during the Battle of Britain.

Above and below: A He 111 of *KG* 55 pictured in a dispersal pen at either Dreux or Chartres during the summer of 1940. The bespoke cockpit and engine covers successfully hide the identity of the variant of this He 111 and whether it is a I or II/*KG* 55 aircraft.

Above: Another view of the He 111 of *KG* 55 with its bespoke cockpit and engine covers, in a dispersal pen at either Dreux or Chartres.

Below: A He 111H of either 1/*KG* 55 or 4/*KG* 55 with its engines running.

Above: A Stab He 111 (indicated by the letters +BA) getting airborne from an unidentified airfield. The unit is either *KG 26* (code 1H) or *KG 27* (1G).

Left: A He 111 of *KG 55* (the unit's griffon emblem is just visible behind the cockpit) photographed in a heavily camouflaged revetment. The identity of the personnel and Gruppe (and therefore airfield) is not known.

Opposite top: An III/*KG 26* He 111H-4, in this case coded 1H+FS, pictured over the North Sea in the summer of 1940. The letter 'F' appears to be red outlined in white. This aircraft was shot down by RAF fighters on 15 August 1940, but its crew, *Oberleutnant* Hermann Riedel (pilot), *Feldwebel* Willi Scholl (Beobachter), *Oberfeldwebel* Paul Süssenbach (Bordfunker) and *Oberfeldwebel* Karl Müller (Bordmechaniker) were eventually rescued none the worse for wear. During the early stages of the Battle of Britain, III/*KG 26* was based at Stavanger in Norway.

Opposite bottom: Preparing a Heinkel He 111 of *KG 55* for a mission as armourers load it with 50kg bombs.

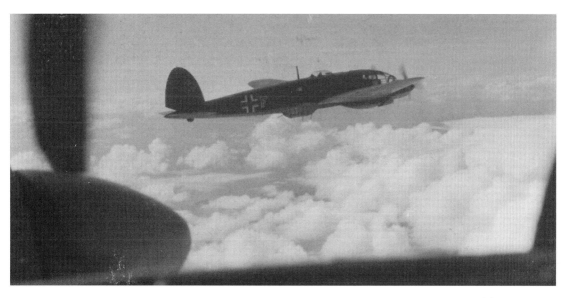

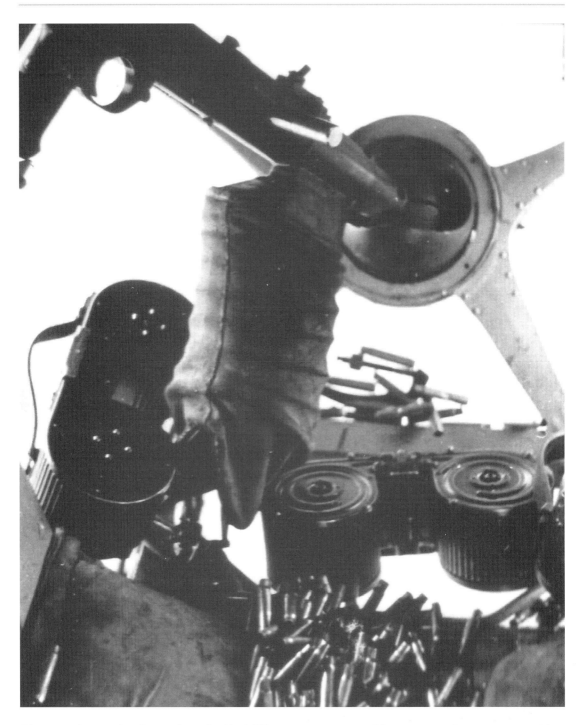

Above and opposite: A member of a He 111's crew clearing up after a mission – a view of the inside of a ventral gondola and one of empty cartridge cases and empty ammunition drums for the MG17 machine-gun lying on the ground.

A He 111 of 1/*KG* 26 seen over the North Sea early in the summer of 1940. The aircraft and crews of 1/*KG* 26 were based at Kristiansand during the early stages of the Battle of Britain.

Below: The wreckage of a He 111H-1 of 1/*Kampfgruppe* 100 on the beach near Hourtin in western France. The unit's characteristic Viking long boat emblem can be seen on the side of the cockpit.

Above and below: It is thought that the Heinkel at Hourtin, commanded by *Leutnant* Oswald Lochbrunner, became lost whilst returning from an attack on the Dunlop Factory in Birmingham and force-landed on the beach in the early hours of 15 August 1940.

Opposite page: Waves lapping at the remains of the Hourtin Heinkel He 111. The aircraft appears to have been coded 6N+DH – the letter 'D' can be seen in white seen on the tail which indicates it to be from 1 Staffel.

Below: The sea gradually broke up and consumed 6N+DH.
The raid on 15 August 1940 cost *Kampfgruppe* 100 at least one other aircraft, 3/*Kampfgruppe* 100's He 111H-3 6N+DL which force-landed near St Brieuc. The crew was unhurt, though the aircraft was a write-off. Another H-3, *werke nummer* 6873, returned damaged after a signal flare accidentally ignited inside the fuselage causing a fire. The Bordschütz, *Unteroffizier* Friedel Dörner, baled out whilst still over the

UK and was captured unhurt at Balcombe in West Sussex. The pilot, *Feldwebel* Kaufmann, was unhurt, whilst *Leutnant* Seebauer and *Feldwebel* Adalbert Knier both suffered slightly burned hands. Their aircraft, 6N+BH, was described as 45% damaged but repairable.

Above: A pair of He 111s from what appears to be *KG* 26 (note the unit emblem on the nose) share a hangar with a Messerschmitt Bf 110C of 9/*Zerstörergeschwader* 76, the latter being coded 2N+EP. It is possible that this photograph was taken immediately after the Battle of Britain as these two units were not co-located during the summer of 1940.

Below: A He 111 of *KG* 26 sits behind a Bf 110D-0 of I/*Zerstörergeschwader* 76 at Stavanger-Sola, August 1940. Both units were badly mauled by RAF fighters whilst attacking north-eastern England on 15 August 1940.

Above: The Heinkel coded A1+AC would normally be the aircraft of the *Gruppen Kommandeur* of II/*KG* 53, who for the early part of the Battle of Britain was *Major* Reinhold Tamm. Tamm would be shot down flying a He 111H-3 by Flying Officer Richard Milne of 151 Squadron, off the Essex coast, on the late afternoon of 18 August 1940. There were no survivors from his crew of *Oberfeldwebel* Kurt Heine (the pilot), *Leutnant* Walter Ludmann (Beobachter), *Oberfeldwebel* Alois Rusch (Bordfunker), *Feldwebel* Erhardt Rasche (Bordmechaniker) and *Gefrieter* Klemens Kahl (Bordschütz).

Right: The wreckage of another He 111H-3 lost on 18 August 1940. Coded V4+GK, this one came from 2/*KG* 1. Flown by *Leutnant* Rudolf Ahrens it was attacked by four Spitfires of 65 Squadron and a Hurricane of 32 Squadron, a combat which caused the oxygen equipment to explode. Ahrens crash-landed at Snargate, near Dymchurch, at 13.40 hours. *Unteroffizier* Helmut Gericke (Bordmechaniker) was mortally wounded, though the rest of the crew, which included *Oberfledwebel* Ernst Katzmarski (Beobachter), *Unteroffizier* Georg Schneider (Bordfunker) and *Flieger* Kurt Natzke (Bordschütz), were all taken prisoner – but not before they set fire to their aircraft.

Above: A He 111 of I/KG 1 pictured over the Thames Estuary early in the afternoon of Sunday, 18 August 1940. This was the hardest fought day of the Battle of Britain, with the Luftwaffe trying its best to destroy the RAF's fighter airfields, undertaking 850 sorties involving 2,200 aircrew. The RAF resisted with equal vigour, flying 927 sorties involving 600 aircrew.

Below: A crew of KG 1 examine the damage inflicted by RAF fighters during a combat in the Battle of Britain. It appears that the He 111 is lying on its belly.

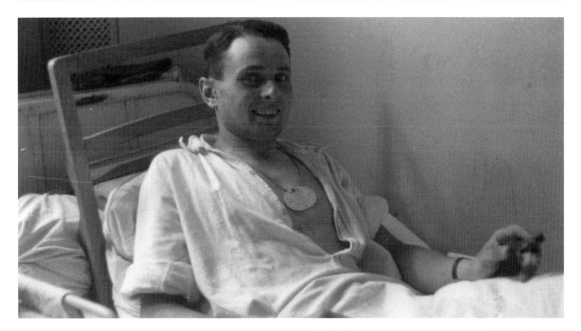

Above: On 11 September 1940, He 111H-3 *werke nummer* 6852 and coded V4+AL of 3/*KG* 1 was damaged by anti-aircraft over London during at attack on the West India Docks. The pilot force-landed at Amiens at 16.30 hours; the aircraft was subsequently found to have suffered 60% damage. The Bordmechaniker, *Feldwebel* Hermann Klammer, was mortally wounded. This photograph shows the Beobachter, *Oberfeldwebel* Hans Welscher, who was wounded in the leg, recuperating in hospital. Welscher recovered from his injuries, only to be killed in an accident on 23 July 1941. At the time he was flying with 9/*KG* 40 (I/*KG* 1 having been re-designated III/*KG* 40 in March 1941) when his He 111H-6, *werke nummer* 4129, crashed west of Bleicherode, south-west of Nordhausen/Harz.

Right: Another wounded crewman from V4+AL. It is the Bordfunker, *Unteroffizier* Willi Berg, who is pictured being treated in hospital after the events of 11 September 1940. Both he and *Oberfeldwebel* Welscher were still in hospital in Amiens a week after the incident. The eventual fate of Willi Berg is not known.

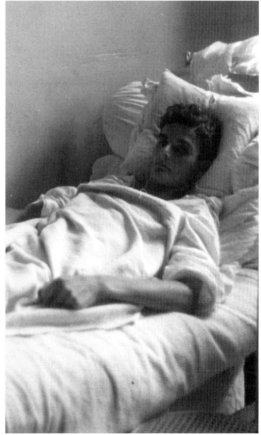

Above and opposite top: *KG* 55 would lose three He 111s attacking Portsmouth on 26 August 1940, with another three returning damaged or with wounded crew. The He 111P-2 seen here, *werke nummer* 2165 and coded G1+GM of 4/*KG* 55, was attacked and damaged by Hurricanes of 43 Squadron. The pilot, *Leutnant* Klaus Walter, managed to carry out a successful crash-landing at Westbrook Farm, Cowplain in Hampshire. The Beobachter, *Oberfeldwebel* Otto Hennecke, was killed; the pilot and the remainder of the crew – *Unteroffizier* Oskar Schufft (Bordfunker), *Unteroffizier* Fritz Marmer (Bordmechaniker) and *Flieger* Josef Wimmer (Bordschütz) – were all captured.

Opposite bottom: Another loss on 26 August 1940 was the He 111P coded G1+BB. A Stab I/*KG* 55 aircraft, it was crippled by RAF fighters and crash-landed at Helyers Farm, Wick near Littlehampton. Two of the crew,

Oberleutnant Ignaz Krenn (pilot) and *Unteroffizier* Helmut Morrack (Beobachter), were captured unwounded, whilst the remainder, *Unteroffizier* Hans Degen (Bordfunker), *Unteroffizier* Willi Schneiders (Bordmechaniker) and *Feldwebel* Alois Schreck (Bordschütz), were all taken prisoner whilst suffering varying degrees of wounds. It would appear that this photograph was taken soon after the He 111 had arrived on *KG* 55 as the manufacturer's codes can still be seen, though they have been overpainted.

Opposite top: On the afternoon of 5 September 1940, this He 111H-2, *werke nummer* 3143 and coded A1+CC of Stab II/*KG* 53, was damaged by fighters during a post-attack reconnaissance of RAF Hornchurch. As these pictures reproduced courtesy of the Schierning family reveal, the pilot, *Oberfeldwebel* Günther Schmidtborn, successfully crash-landed at Lille-Vendeville.

Opposite bottom: Schmidtborn, on the right smoking the cigarette, and members of his crew pose in front of A1+CC at Lille-Vendeville. The individual standing to Schmidtborn's right, pointing at a bullet hole in the spinner, is the Beobachter, *Oberleutnant* Hans-Peter Schierning. The other crew members were Bordmechaniker *Unteroffizier* Eugen Schilling, *Unteroffizier* Max Nagl (Bordfunker) and *Gefrieter* Joachim Kupfer (Bordschütz). They were all uninjured apart from Kupfer.

Above: Another view of A1+CC after its crash-landing on 5 September 1940, the ambulance having arrived to tend to Kupfer. Ten days later, Schmidtborn's crew, minus Kupfer who was replaced by *Feldwebel* Andreas Grassl, together with *Major* Max Grüber (*Gruppen Kommandeur*), was shot down by Spitfires of 92 Squadron whilst flying a He 111H-3 coded A1+GM (*werke nummer* 6843). Schmidtborn once again managed to effect a crash-landing, though this time at Frittenden in Kent. All but Grassl, who was killed, were captured.

Above: Taken by another Luftwaffe aircraft at 18.48 hours (German time) on 7 September 1940, the identity of this He 111 has never been ascertained but the location is without doubt – directly over Wapping and Rotherhithe.

Above and below: Another Battle of Britain casualty. All that can be ascertained from this image is the fact that the 'A1+' code identifies this He 111P as being from *KG* 53, whilst the white spinners denote 1, 4 or 7 Staffeln. It would appear that the aircraft has suffered a landing accident which has caused the port undercarriage to collapse.

Above: A view of the cockpit of a Stab III/*KG* 53 He 111. To the right, at the controls, is *Feldwebel* Oskar Broderix who would be taken prisoner of war on 9 September 1940.

Opposite top: Oskar Broderix also appears in this group photograph of *KG* 53 personnel, albeit with the rank of *Oberfeldwebel*. He can be seen standing on the far right. The other men, from left to right, are *Feldwebel* Ernst Wendorf (Bordfunker), *Feldwebel* Willi Wenninger (Bordmechaniker) and *Oberleutnant* Kurt Meinecke (Beobachter). They are standing in front of a brand new He 111H-2, *werke nummer* 2630 and coded A1+ZD, of Stab III/*KG* 53. On 9 September 1940 this aircraft collided with the Hurricane of 605 Squadron flown by Pilot Officer George Forrester; the He 111 crashed near Chawton in Hampshire. Meinecke and Broderix were the only survivors. Forrester was also killed, as was *Feldwebel* Willi Döring (Bordschütz).

Opposite bottom: Officers of II/*KG* 53 seen at Nordwyck for the departure of their *Gruppen Kommandeur*, *Oberstleutnant* Wilhlem Kohlbach. Second from the right is *Oberleutnant* Dietrich von Buttlar. He would command 6/*KG* 53 and gain prominence for his part in an attack on the Rolls-Royce factory in Derby on 29 September 1940 whilst with 1/*KG* 53. Von Buttlar was killed on 7 May 1943 whilst commanding 2/*KG* 6.

Above: The view looking forward from the bomb bay of a He 111 of *Kampfgruppe* 100.

Note the control column to the left and the area where the Beobachter would lie to the right.

Above and below: A He 111H of II/*KG 26* pictured having been prepared for night operations - its engines are running in one of the shots. The aircraft's markings have been toned down and it is carrying a 500 kg bomb externally. This photograph is believed to have been taken at Amiens towards the end of the Battle of Britain.

Above: A He 111H of *Kampfgruppe* 100 pictured with an unidentified crew. Note the distemper on the under surfaces and last two digits of the *werke nummer* on the nose. Between these digits and the unit emblem is the fuel octane triangle.

Opposite top: A He 111H of 4/*KG* 55. It is possible that the aircraft seen here is a replacement for the He 111P-2 coded G1+GM (*werke nummer* 2165) which was shot down near Portsmouth on 26 August 1940.

Opposite bottom: This He 111H-3 of 4/*KG* 53, *werke nummer* 5560 and coded A1+LM, suffered radio failure whilst on a night mission over the UK on 28 August 1940. The crew then became lost, finally belly landing at Wullach

near Wesel in Germany. The aircraft was categorised as being 50% damaged. Note the hastily toned-down white spinners and tail swastika.

Opposite top and bottom: This *KG 26* He
111H has suffered a taxiing accident, having
struck a parked vehicle. The photograph
was taken in Norway, probably early in the
Battle of Britain, and the bomber is thought
to have come from 1/*KG 26*. I/*KG 26* moved
to Beauvais in France in September 1940.

Above: This He 111P-2 of 9/*KG* 55, *werke
nummer* 3354 and coded G1+LT, crashed
and was destroyed at Villacoublay whilst
taking off for an attack on London on 8
December 1940. The crew, *Leutnant* Walter
Lehenbauer (pilot), *Unteroffizier* Heinz
Herrmann (Beobachter), *Feldwebel* Gottfried
Schreier (Bordfunker) and *Feldwebel* Karl
Ries (Bordmechaniker), were all killed.

Opposite: *Major* Viktor von Lossberg, seen here at the controls of a He 111, took command of III/*KG* 26 in November 1939, before moving to a staff appointment with Luftflotte 2 at the start of June 1940. He resumed command in February 1941 by which time III/*KG* 26 was operating Y Gerät. He would remain with III/*KG* 26 until September 1941, being awarded the Ritterkreuz the following month. A series of staff appointments followed during which time he flew thirty-nine night fighter sorties. He passed away in 1983.

Below: A Heinkel 111H-5 of Stab III/*KG* 26 pictured just before taking off on a raid to bomb a target in Britain during the Blitz. Note the distinctive Y-*Verfahren* aerial that can be seen just behind the pilot, *Major* Viktor von Lossberg.

Opposite top: Coded 1G+IK, this is a He 111 of 2/*KG* 27. This unit was based at Avord, Tours, Bourges, Rennes, Orleans and Dinard for the Battle of Britain and Blitz before moving east in June 1941.

Opposite bottom: Flown by *Feldwebel* Fritz Jürges, who was briefed to attack Bristol, this He 111H-3 of 1/*KG* 55, *werke nummer* 6305 and coded G1+BH, was shot down by Spitfires of 609 Squadron and a Hurricane of 238 Squadron on the afternoon of 25 September 1940. *Gefrieter* Rudolf Weissbach, Jürges' Bordfunker, later provided this account: 'After we had dropped our bombs, we saw the first Spitfire, and they attacked immediately. During one of the attacks we lost an engine (the oil supply was hit), and then could not set the pitch of the propeller.

We were flying in formation at 5,000m and could not keep up so we dropped as much ballast as possible in the hope that we could reach the French coast on one engine.' The crew's efforts were in vain, however, and Jürges crash-landed at Westland Farm, Ballard Down, Swanage in Dorset.

Above: A close-up of the cockpit of Jürges' Heinkel at Westland Farm. The aircraft's camouflage was described as 'dark green all over with lamp black on the under-surfaces and covering white spinners'. The latter can be noted in this shot. Jürges and Weissbach were both captured, as were *Hauptmann* Karl Köthke (Beobachter) and *Flieger* Otto Müller (Bordschütz). The final crewman, *Gefrieter* Josef Altrichter (Bordmechaniker), had been mortally wounded.

Opposite top: Another view of the wreckage of G1+BH. Ahead of the 'G1' code on the port side is the distinctive white buffalo emblem, similar to other artwork seen on I/*KG* 55 aircraft, which was designed by 1 Staffel's *Hauptmann* Arthur von Casimir. A subsequent RAF intelligence report noted that 'following fighter action, the starboard engine was hit and burst of .303 are shown half way down fuselage and in wings. Aircraft landed with undercarriage retracted and is reported to be in good condition.'

Opposite bottom: Another emblem seen on a 3/*KG* 55 He 111. The crewman in this image, Bordfunker *Unteroffizier* Hans Schade, is believed to have been killed in action on 27 July 1943. Serving with Stab III/*KG* 55 at the time, his He 111H-1, *werke nummer* 110085 and coded G1+AD, was damaged by a Soviet night fighter twenty miles north-west of Bataisk.

Above: By the end of the Battle of Britain, *Kampfgruppe* 100 was flying all of its missions by night. This is probably the He 111H-3 coded 6N+DH of 1 Staffel.

Above: This is the He 111P of Stab/*KG* 55 which, coded G1+FA, was shot down by 43 Squadron on 12 July 1940. Flown by *Feldwebel* John Möhn, it crash-landed near the Horse and Jockey Inn at Hipley, Hampshire, at 16.30 hours. Möhn was captured, as were *Feldwebel* Heinz Kalina (Bordfunker), *Oberfeldwebel* Fritz Knecht (Bordmechaniker) and *Oberfeldwebel* Philipp Müller (Bordschütz) captured; *Oberleutnant* Walter Kleinhanns (Beobachter) was killed.

Möhn had been previously wounded in action, when he and his crew (which at the time also included Kalina and Knecht) were attacked by pilots of *Groupe de Chasse* II/2 near Montage du Larmont on 15 May 1940 during a mission to Dijon. Möhn force-landed

near Freiburg. As well as Möhn, Kalina, Knecht, *Feldwebel* Heinz Scheithauer (Beobachter), and *Unteroffizier* Werner Abbinghoff (Bordschütz) were also all wounded. Scheithauer was commissioned, only to be killed in an accident with 7 Staffel on 28 August 1940.

Opposite top: A He 111 of III/*KG* 27 getting airborne from Rennes in the summer of 1940. III/*KG* 27 was based in Avord, Rennes and finally, from 23 March 1941, Orleans-Bricy.

Opposite bottom: This silhouetted He 111 would be difficult to identify were it not for the three aerials indicating it was fitted with X Gerät and is therefore from *Kampfgruppe* 100.

Opposite top: A He 111H of *Kampfgruppe* 100 photographed taking off from Vannes in the summer of 1940.

Opposite bottom: A He 111 of *KG* 55 setting out on a night mission in the autumn of 1940. Note it carries a 500kg bomb externally.

Above: He 111 H 6N+EK of 2/ *Kampfgruppe* 100 on the compass swinging base at Vannes. As normal with *Kampfgruppe* 100's He 111s, it has the individual letter on the tip of the tail, in this case a red E.

For the Luftwaffe, night operations on the evening of Saturday, 9 November 1940, began earlier than had been the case over the previous nights. The air raid sirens in the Borough of Bromley sounded about 19.00 hours. Just half an hour later disaster struck. En route to central London, a Heinkel He 111H of 2/KG 21, *werke nummer* 3335 and coded V4+JK, was hit by anti-aircraft fire. The damage was so severe that the bomber broke up in the air. One of the wings, severed from the rest of the fuselage, fell away and fluttered down to earth, landing in the garden at the rear of 45 Cranmore Road, West Chislehurst.

With his aircraft out of control, the pilot,

Leutnant Max Probst baled out. He was followed by one of his crew. Moments later, at 19.28 hours, the Heinkel slammed into the ground near Bromley Common, demolishing a pair of houses – Nos. 26 and 28 Johnson Road.

Two of the Heinkel's crew were still inside the aircraft. *Leutnant* Probst, meanwhile, landed in the grounds of the Sundridge Park Hotel where he was detained by staff. The fourth member of the plane's crew had baled out too late for his parachute to open fully and he had struck the roof of 14 Johnson Road. He hung mortally wounded down the side of the house, his parachute entangled in its chimney. It was reported that he died from his wounds shortly after being cut down and taken to hospital.

There were also casualties amongst the occupants of the properties struck by the main section of V4+JK. Thirty-one-year-old Alice Evelyn Monday, who lived at No.26 with her husband H.A. Monday, had been killed outright. Six others, all badly injured, lay trapped in the wreckage.

Rescue workers were quickly on the scene, only to discover that between them and the trapped civilians was the Heinkel's full bomb load of some 30 SC-50 bombs – all of which had not exploded. One of those who arrived at Johnson Road was Police Sergeant David Lionel Grigg, a Traffic Patrol Officer of the Metropolitan Police's 'P' Division at Catford. The following account, published in *The London Gazette*, gives some indication of what followed:

'Four persons were rescued, slightly injured. Shortly afterwards, four more bombs were dropped nearby, only a few yards from the Police and Rescue Parties, causing them to suspend operations for a few minutes. When the rescue work was resumed, it was discovered that a number of bombs, several of which were still attached to parts of the machine, were amongst the debris. Two more

persons were trapped underneath and it was necessary to remove the bombs before they could be extricated.

'Police Sergeant Grigg volunteered to carry the bombs from the wrecked houses and removed three of them from the wreckage.' These he carried across the main A.21 Hastings Road to open ground.

'He was about to return for a fourth,' continues the account, 'when it was suspected that one or more were about to explode. Nevertheless, Grigg again entered the wreckage and removed the bomb. The Sergeant then crawled beneath the debris and located one of the trapped victims, who was eventually rescued.'

During this no-doubt tense and seemingly endless procedure, other rescuers set out to alleviate the suffering of those still trapped. Having been Bromley's Medical Officer of Health since 1926, Dr Kenneth Edwin Tapper OBE was also the head of the Borough's ARP Casualty Services.

As Sergeant Grigg toiled with the unexploded bombs, one of which was stated to have been ticking as he lugged it from the scene, Tapper crawled under the debris and wreckage to reach the casualties, oblivious to the risk he was taking.

Sergeant Grigg, *The London Gazette* added, 'showed great courage and devotion to duty'. For his part, Dr Tapper had 'shown great gallantry in his efforts to relieve suffering amongst air raid victims'. It was noted that he had "on many occasions during enemy air attacks crawled under wreckage to search for and give treatment to injured casualties pinned down by debris'. For their efforts that night, both Sergeant Grigg and Dr Tapper were awarded the George Medal.

The image seen here shows rescuers still hard at work amongst the wreckage of Nos. 26 and 28 Johnson Road – note the unexploded bomb being carried from the debris. Both properties have since been rebuilt.

Opposite top: The He 111 crew of
Feldwebel Kurt Braun (Bordmechaniker),
Oberfeldwebel Paul Wierbitzky (pilot),
Oberfeldwebel Hilmar Schmidt (Beobachter)
and *Unteroffizier* Herbert Schick
(Bordfunker). Whilst this crew was both
successful and experienced, its luck ran out
on during an attack on Chatham, Kent, on
14 June 1941.
On this date its He 111H-3, *werke nummer*
5652 and coded 6N+FK (a replacement
aircraft for the one seen in this photograph),
was shot down by a Bristol Beaufighter of
219 Squadron and crashed at Guestling in
Sussex. All were taken prisoner.

Opposite bottom: *Unteroffizier* Herbert
Schick sitting astride the He 111H-1 coded
6N+FK (*werke nummer* 5102). Note the
letter 'F' is white when it should be black or
red for 2 Staffel.

Above: This He 111P coded G1+BS of 8/*KG*
55 has been painted for nocturnal missions,
though the unit's three fishes emblem is still
visible, this time painted in a shield. It is
probable that this is the He 111P-2 with the
werke nummer 2809 which was damaged by
anti-aircraft fire on the evening of 8 October
1940. It returned to Villacoublay with two of
the crew, *Unteroffizier* Herbert Heinzel
(Beobachter) and *Unteroffizier* Josef Bogner
(Bordschütz), wounded.

Opposite top: The aircraft of 8/*KG* 55 (commanded by *Hauptmann* Karl-Egon Knauer until the start of August 1940, *Hauptmann* Heinrich Wittmer until 30 September 1940, and then *Oberleutnant* Jürgen Bartens) carried an emblem of three small fishes on the rudder – an insignia which can be seen on this He 111P.

Opposite bottom: A He 111 H of *KG* 27 (the partial code '1G' is just visible ahead of the cross) has tipped in its nose after its starboard wheel has hit soft earth. The toning down of both camouflage and markings is very obvious on this aircraft.

Below: The *werke nummer* 2626 on this aircraft identifies it as the He 111P-2 coded 1G+IT of 9/*KG* 27. In the early hours of 22 October 1940, following a mission over the

UK, the pilot, *Leutnant* Rudolf Jansen, crashed into a lake less than a mile south of Goven whilst trying to land at Rennes in fog. Jansen and *Unteroffizier* Erwin-Oskar Schmidt were killed, as were *Feldwebel* Max Karwinkel from 7 Staffel and the *Gruppen Kommandeur* of III/*KG* 27, *Major* Manfred Freiherr Speck von Sternburg. *Feldwebel* Gerhard Hobbie jumped without a parachute but survived, albeit badly injured. *Hauptmann* Hans-Henning von Beust duly took over as commander of III/*KG* 27, his place as the Staffel Kapitän of 7/*KG* 27 being filled by *Oberleutnant* Erich Thiel.

Both von Beust and Thiel would receive the Ritterkreuz, the former also receiving the Oakleaves. Thiel was killed in action over the Soviet Union on 22 April 1943; Von Beust passed away in 1991.

Above: One of the most successful Heinkel He 111 pilots of the Battle of Britain was *Leutnant* Johann 'Hans' Thurner of 9/*KG* 55 – seen here on the right with fellow crew members. Joining his Staffel at Villacoublay at the start of the Battle of Britain, Thurner quickly proved himself to be a gifted pilot, he and his crew specialising in attacking important targets such as the Westland aircraft factory at Yeovil and the Birmetals factory at Birmingham. By 13 April 1941, he had qualified for the Operational Mission Clasp in Silver for sixty missions and on 25 June 1941, at the start of the war in Russia, the Mission Clasp in Gold for 110 missions. He also received the Honour Goblet on 17 May 1941.

Opposite: Another view of Johann 'Hans' Thurner at the controls of a Heinkel He 111. On the second day of operations in Russia,

Thurner's bomber was damaged by anti-aircraft fire whilst attacking troops near Wlodzimierz-Luck and his Beobachter, *Unteroffizier* Alois Heugenhäuser, was killed and Bordschütz *Gefrieter* Erich Engler wounded; he and the remainder of his crew (*Feldwebel* Herbert Pottlkämper and *Feldwebel* Werner Heinde) were uninjured. Two days later, Thurner flew 150 miles back to base on one engine after having suffered further Flak damage attacking a railway line at Kowel.

However, his luck ran out on 2 July 1941 when he was wounded by ground fire near Luck; he did not return to operational flying until September 1941. On 6 August 1941, Thurner was awarded the Knights Cross for his achievements. He would be awarded the Oakleaves but was killed in action commanding I/*KG* 6 over Normandy on 10 June 1944.

Above: An atmospheric shot of a group of Heinkel He 111s at a Luftwaffe airfield in France preparing for a night mission during the Blitz in 1941.

Opposite top: A photograph of what is believed to the Heinkel He 111 of *Oberfeldwebel* Herbert Rose of Stab III/*KG* 26, *werke* number 3595 (note the '95' on the nose), being pushed back into a revetment at le Bourget, 11 February 1941. Rose and his crew were shot down on the night of 4 April 1941, during a raid on Avonmouth. The victor, a Bristol Beaufighter of 604 (County of Middlesex) Squadron, caused Rose to crash at West Hewish, Weston-Super-Mare. Rose and

two others survived and were captured; two other crewmen were killed.

Opposite bottom: The burnt out wreckage of another *KG* 26 loss, in this case Heinkel He 111H-5 *werke* number 3592, lying where it came to a halt on Blatchington Golf Course, near Seaford in East Sussex, at about 22.00 hours on the evening of Thursday, 10 April 1941. Note what may be anti-invasion wires in the background. With *Leutnant* Claus Conrad at the controls, this bomber had taken off from Paris Le Bourget to attack industrial targets in Birmingham. It was, however, intercepted by a 264 Squadron Boulton Paul Defiant flown by Flying Officer Eric Barwell.

Left: *Leutnant* Claus Conrad at the controls of a Heinkel He 111 – though it is not known if it is the same aircraft he was flying on the night of 10-11 April 1941. The only member of Conrad's Heinkel who was killed was his Beobachter, *Oberfeldwebel* Hermann Platt, who was killed when his parachute failed to open fully. Conrad later stated: 'Unfortunately he must have hit the tail unit losing consciousness. Later I was told that he had not pulled the ripcord and was killed instantly when he hit the ground.'

Below: Deputy Führer Rudolph Hess pays a visit to III/*KG* 55 at Villacoublay, 23 December 1940. From this point on, operations would become increasingly difficult for *KG* 55 and its crews as the Luftwaffe turned its eyes eastwards and southwards, rather than just at Great Britain.